LE

the

PROMISES OF GOD

for

MEN

TONY DUNGY
AND NATHAN WHITAKER

The Tyndale nonfiction imprint

Visit Tyndale online at tyndale.com.

Visit Tyndale Momentum online at tyndalemomentum.com.

TYNDALE, Tyndale's quill logo, *Tyndale Momentum*, and the Tyndale Momentum logo are registered trademarks of Tyndale House Ministries. Tyndale Momentum is the nonfiction imprint of Tyndale House Publishers, Carol Stream, Illinois.

Designed by Dean H. Renninger and Libby Dykstra

Edited by Bonne L. Steffen

Published in association with the literary agency of Legacy, LLC, Winter Park, Florida 32789.

For information about special discounts for bulk purchases, please contact Tyndale House Publishers at csresponse@tyndale.com, or call 1-855-277-9400.

ISBN 978-1-4964-5099-9

Printed in the United States of America

27	26	25	24	23	22	21
7	6	5	4	3	2	1

Leaning on the Promises of God for Men

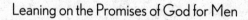

Because of his glory and excellence, he has given us great and precious promises. These are the promises that enable you to share his divine nature and escape the world's corruption caused by human desires.

2 PETER 1:4

A Note from the Coach

Men today get pulled in every direction by people and society. Everyone has a different expectation for us: be a provider, be tough, be sensitive, don't cry, stay home, go to work, change diapers, go hang out with the boys, *don't* go hang out with the boys, and so on.

Some have said that being a man today means to be sensitive and caring, to be nurturing, quick to comfort, open to talk. Still others have said that we've been created to explore caves and beat our chests in some sort of masculine cosmic rhythm.

It's easy to get swept along, borne by the current with no idea where you're headed. Sometimes you find yourself miles out from shore with the lighthouse no longer visible. I've seen it over and over through the years, and I've even felt the pull myself. There have been plenty of times when I've looked around and wondered, *Now, how did I get here? Where is here? And who are these people floating alongside me?*

Unfortunately, that seems to be the path that way too many of us naturally take. A world in which things are accepted as normal without any thought as to whether they should be, or that there might be a better way. Too often we resign ourselves to accepting that things just *are* the way they are.

In football, when our team isn't playing well, I might say, "We have to get back to our fundamentals," referring to those basic principles that allow us to play the game successfully—blocking, tackling, running, catching.

We need to get back to the fundamentals as men as well. The basic principles found there will allow us to succeed as men. We can be certain there will always be obstacles along the way. However, having the fundamentals to fall back on will help us to overcome those obstacles.

And for me, most—if not *all*—of those fundamentals are firmly rooted in Scripture.

In fact, I cannot think of a better playbook to help you navigate the game of life.

While I don't pretend to have all the answers, I hope this little book will help ground you in your daily interactions, provide encouragement when life gets difficult, and help you think about where you're headed and who you want to be.

Because the simple truth is, you *can* be more. In fact, you were *created* to be more.

Tony Dungy

A PERSONAL TRAINING PLAN

Self-control. Discipline. Getting in shape.

How many times have you written down these goals when committing to a new program of self-improvement? In a CNN report, it wasn't surprising to learn that losing weight is the most common goal people set. And then we come to our senses—about a month later.

When I was a player, professional football wasn't a year-round enterprise, and when camp began, some guys would show up totally out of shape.

As followers of Christ, we should maintain self-control and discipline, especially when it comes to taking care of our bodies. Getting in shape and making a commitment to stay that way honors God. He has given us our bodies through the miracle of creation. Taking care of them, watching what we put into them, and being careful about how we use them each day are responsibilities we shouldn't take lightly.

But that mindset is not only important for our physical bodies. That desire and discipline also apply to the training we do and the commitment we make to ourselves and to God. We commit to learn more about Him and about how we can be better disciples. It's not a passive endeavor. It takes resolve and repetition, consistently working at it for maximum results. And results will happen as we grow closer to Him.

Real success in achieving goals—no matter when we set them—comes when we know we can't do it by ourselves and look to the Lord for strength.

His Promises

No discipline is enjoyable while it is happening—it's painful! But afterward there will be a peaceful harvest of right living for those who are trained in this way.

HEBREWS 12:11

God has not given us a spirit of fear and timidity, but of power, love, and self-discipline.

2 TIMOTHY 1:7

All athletes are disciplined in their training. They do it to win a prize that will fade away, but we do it for an eternal prize.

1 CORINTHIANS 9:25

KEEP YOUR
ANGER IN CHECK

We've all been tempted to do it, even on a small scale. We want to get back at someone for something they've done with a snide remark or by criticizing them in front of others. If we haven't done it, at least we've thought about doing it. In either case, it only makes the original issue worse. Once anger, frustration, deceit, or cunning ways get a foothold in any situation in our lives, the devil begins to have a field day. There is no telling when we will be able to turn things around, restore the relationship—if ever—or regain our reputation.

No matter what happens to you, don't compound the problem by trying to get back at whoever did something to you. So often it's not the initial issue or incident that gets you into trouble—it's what happens next. Think about it.

How often have you seen the player who retaliates for a cheap shot get the penalty flag thrown on him instead of on the original offender?

It happens all the time in football, and it happens all the time in life. A friend or a spouse says something, and we retaliate angrily. God doesn't think in terms of who said what first or how sinful one person's actions may be when compared with another's. All sin causes a person to be separated from God because God is holy, He cannot look at sin, no matter how small or how heinous it is.

When you find yourself in a volatile situation, don't make things worse by letting anger get the better of you. Be wiser than hot-tempered people with short fuses. If you stay calm instead of reacting angrily, it will be easier to control yourself in whatever situation you find yourself. And it may have a lasting effect on someone else.

His Promises

Fools vent their anger,
but the wise quietly hold it back.

PROVERBS 29:11

Don't repay evil for evil. Don't retaliate with insults when people insult you. Instead, pay them back with a blessing. That is what God has called you to do, and he will grant you his blessing.

1 PETER 3:9

Whoever is slow to anger is better than the mighty,
and he who rules his spirit than he who takes a city.

PROVERBS 16:32, ESV

CONTRARY TO POPULAR OPINION

Popular culture sends us a lot of messages about value and worth. In magazines, music, television shows, movies, sports, and any other form of entertainment, we are continually told that the respect we receive depends on the status we have—and that status is defined by wealth, style, or popular opinion.

We not only begin to evaluate ourselves that way, we evaluate others that way too. If they don't work a certain kind of job, earn a certain level of income, dress a certain way, or have a lifestyle we envy, they probably aren't successful. And if they aren't successful, they aren't significant or worthy of our attention.

But real significance isn't defined by popular culture. In fact, culture often magnifies less significant things and minimizes truly significant things. We can spend our entire lives going down that path, trying to find true significance in things that can never give it to us.

The Bible tells us what true significance is, and it isn't found in what we have, in the status we attain, or even in what we accomplish. It's found in knowing God, living faithfully for Him, loving Him and others, and doing whatever He has called us to do—even if it doesn't impress anyone else. It's about our identity in Him, not our achievements and possessions.

We have worth not because of what we do and have but because we are His children and He chooses to love us. Our worth doesn't depend on us; it's based on how He values us. And He values us simply because He made us and we belong to Him.

His Promises

He saved us, not because of the righteous things we had done, but because of his mercy. He washed away our sins, giving us a new birth and new life through the Holy Spirit.

TITUS 3:5

"For I know the plans I have for you," says the
LORD. *"They are plans for good and not for
disaster, to give you a future and a hope."*
JEREMIAH 29:11

*Take delight in the LORD,
    and he will give you your heart's desires.*
PSALM 37:4

MEEK
DOESN'T = WEAK

The Jews who lived in Jesus' day had been eagerly anticipating the Messiah as the fulfillment of Isaiah's prophecy of "the Spirit of the Sovereign LORD."

But none of them anticipated the Messiah would be a humble and meek person. Meekness wasn't a common trait found in a powerful leader. Nor is it the first word you might use to characterize a professional athlete who relies on strength, speed, toughness, confidence, and—at times—cockiness to be able to excel.

And yet meekness is the very character trait that we all should have.

Meek people realize their position before God and gladly live it out before their fellow human beings. They do not look down on themselves, but they do not think too highly of themselves either. Their focus remains on God. They know their gifts and abilities come from God. They remember that where they want to be is standing before a Holy God, available to Him, allowing Him to flow and work through them for His glory, not for self or societal adulation. They don't carry a microphone around with them to tell others of their deeds.

The spirit of meekness before God is found in the Spirit of Christ, who gave His life as a sacrifice for you and for me. Clearly, the meekness Jesus displays is not weakness, but a strength to aspire to make our own.

His Promises

God blesses those who are humble,
for they will inherit the whole earth.
MATTHEW 5:5

Humble yourselves before the Lord, and he will
life you up in honor.
JAMES 4:10

He leads the humble in what is right,
and teaches the humble his way.
PSALM 25:9, ESV

EVERYONE'S
A CRITIC

Some people are incessant critics.

The Pharisees and Sadducees criticized John the Baptist for not drinking wine or eating enough, and they criticized Jesus for eating and drinking with tax collectors, prostitutes, and other sinners. They didn't like what John and Jesus stood for, so they did all they could to find things to criticize them about and damage their credibility in the eyes of the general public.

I've faced that at times—we all do. I've received criticism for having a defense-led team in Tampa Bay rather than developing a higher-powered offense; then in Indianapolis, I was criticized for having an offensive-minded team that didn't have enough defensive stars.

Some criticize NFL coaches for making the

playoffs regularly but never "winning the big one." Other coaches are criticized for selling out their future teams to attempt one year of greatness instead of regular appearances in the playoffs.

Go figure.

That's what Jesus noted too. People criticized John for *not* drinking wine and then criticized Jesus *for* drinking wine. Of course, the religious leaders of the day criticized both of them for other things as well—revealing the inconsistency in their complaints.

When people criticize you, it's not always for your actions; sometimes it's for what you represent. If they're really criticizing you for your faith, it's important to maintain your focus and continue on the pathway that God has set before you, even in the midst of criticism.

His Promises

Let us think of ways to motivate one another to acts of love and good works.
HEBREWS 10:24

Encourage each other and build each other up, just as you are already doing.
1 THESSALONIANS 5:11

Don't copy the behavior and customs of this world, but let God transform you into a new person by changing the way you think. Then you will learn to know God's will for you, which is good and pleasing and perfect.

ROMANS 12:2

WATCH YOURSELF

How often have you seen someone blowing his own horn—or trying to—only to have it blow up in his face?

It happens on a regular basis in the world of sports. There's the player who brags before the game about a sure victory because his performance alone will make it happen, and then he has one of his worst games ever. Or the player who is showboating in the middle of a play, high stepping it toward the end zone after badly beating the defensive coverage on a long pass play, and he drops the ball just before he crosses over the goal line into the end zone. No touchdown.

In Luke 18:9-14, Jesus describes an incident of showboating in the story of the praying Pharisee and the tax collector. Both men were in the Temple. The Pharisee, a religious leader, thanked God that he wasn't a sinner like the other people around him. The tax collector, on the other hand, lamented his sins with regret to God. To the astonishment of his listeners, Jesus says it is the tax collector who is justified before God, not the Pharisee. Then He concludes by saying, "Those who exalt themselves will be humbled, and those who humble themselves will be exalted" (verse 14).

Have you caught yourself saying or doing something with an intentional "look at me" attitude? It can happen to anyone. And so can falling flat on your face and eating humble pie.

His Promises

Those who exalt themselves will be humbled, and those who humble themselves will be exalted.

MATTHEW 23:12

Pride ends in humiliation,
while humility brings honor.

PROVERBS 29:23

If you think you are too important to help someone, you are only fooling yourself.

GALATIANS 6:3

HONESTY REALLY IS THE BEST POLICY

I know a man who used to work in the front office of several teams in the NFL, rising as high as vice president for one. He was the business equivalent of the "five-tool player" in baseball: he was extremely bright; well educated; comfortable dealing with players, business leaders, coaches, and fans; and was a great ambassador for the team and the league. He quickly grasped the issues facing the league, navigated his team through competitive challenges, and built a strong product for his team's owner, both on and off the field.

There were many observers around the league who anticipated that he might eventually end up as the next commissioner of the NFL.

He's now out of the league completely. What happened?

Sadly, he had a hang-up with honesty. He simply couldn't tell the truth. It got to the point where, on occasion, he even joked about it. Ultimately, however, that character flaw proved to be his undoing, outweighing any assets he brought with him. When people can't rely on your word, when they can't trust you, it undermines everything else you are trying to do.

Honesty is a component of a person's character that is remembered far longer than an individual's words, talents, or accomplishments. All those things can carry a person to a point, but ultimately, without honing that deep core of honesty, they will all be for naught.

Be someone who tells the truth. Let your "yes" be "yes." Nothing more and nothing less.

His Promises

Just say a simple, "Yes, I will," or "No, I won't." Anything beyond this is from the evil one.

MATTHEW 5:37

*Better to be poor and honest
than to be dishonest and a fool.*

PROVERBS 19:1

If you want to enjoy life
and see many happy days,
keep your tongue from speaking evil
and your lips from telling lies.
Turn away from evil and do good.
Search for peace, and work to maintain it.
The eyes of the LORD watch over those who do
right,
and his ears are open to their prayers.
But the LORD turns his face
against those who do evil.

1 PETER 3:10-12

GETTING IT DONE

We all know them. We don't see them every day, but we still need them. They are the people in the background who take care of the things that wouldn't happen without their help. Great coaches and good leaders recognize their importance—those essential members of the team who get things done, often quietly working in the backrooms and behind the scenes. They are invaluable and indispensable people.

The only time you're aware that someone is running the PowerPoint display for a worship service or for a business conference is when it stops working. But your praise and worship service might have less impact without the technician's contributions. The evaluations at the end of your business meetings might fall short of expectations if the material and presentation relied solely on you to pull it off.

In football, fans watch cornerbacks make spectacular plays to break up passes, and revel in their abilities, but they often miss the great job the cornerback on the other side of the field is doing because the quarterback never throws to the wide receiver on that side. But the coach notices and knows the team cannot win without him.

From time to time, thank the unheralded people on your team, in your work environment, at school, or even at home. Maybe they intentionally avoid the spotlight, but you'd be lost without them. Their skills make you the best you can be. Never take them for granted. God appreciates those who do their work for Him without seeking any glory.

His Promises

Work with enthusiasm, as though you were working for the Lord rather than for people. Remember that the Lord will reward each one of us for the good we do.

EPHESIANS 6:7-8

Make it your goal to live a quiet life, minding your own business and working with your hands, just as we instructed you before. Then people who are not believers will respect the way you live, and you will not need to depend on others.

1 THESSALONIANS 4:11-12

Whatever you do, do well.

ECCLESIASTES 9:10

KEEP IT CLEAN

I've always heard that foul language is not only tolerated in football locker rooms and on the field, it's expected.

But the way I see it, using abusive language toward officials will only get your team penalized or get you ejected from the game. The same language, if used in a television interview, would draw a fine, suspension, or firing.

If you use foul language on a regular basis and brush it off as "I'm just kidding around," people will lose their trust in you and it could damage relationships forever. They won't know whether they can trust you enough to bring something serious for your counsel or input.

What do you do when someone hurts you by saying mean things? If it is directed personally toward me, I can handle it easier than if someone hurts or tries to hurt someone I love. In that case, my first instinct is for the gloves to come off. My better instincts cause me to wrap my loved one within my protective embrace and try not to make the situation worse by lowering myself to the same level of bitterness, harshness, anger, or slander being thrown at them.

None of this is easy to do. In fact, we have to ask Christ to control our thoughts, words, responses, and behavior. When we do, we bring honor and glory to Him—for all of the world to see.

His Promises

Don't use foul or abusive language. . . . Get rid of all bitterness, rage, anger, harsh words, and slander, as well as all types of evil behavior.
EPHESIANS 4:29, 31

Obscene stories, foolish talk, and coarse jokes— these are not for you. Instead, let there be thankfulness to God. You can be sure that no immoral, impure, or greedy person will inherit the Kingdom of Christ and of God.
EPHESIANS 5:4-5

A good person produces good things from the treasury of a good heart, and an evil person produces evil things from the treasury of an evil heart. What you say flows from what is in your heart.

LUKE 6:45

LIVE WITH INTEGRITY

When I was appointed to the President's Council on Service and Civic Participation, the FBI did a background check on me and the other appointees. We had to answer a lot of questions, but the last one really made me think: "Have you ever done anything that would be embarrassing for the president of the United States to be associated with?" It's an interesting thought—that my behavior throughout the course of my life could have an impact on someone else's reputation. It made me wish I had worked a little harder in the area of integrity.

None of us are perfect, but we can be authentic, grow in character, and live in a way that causes people to trust us and want to associate with us. Whether we have integrity or not may be a very personal decision—actually a constant stream of decisions—but it always affects others. Our minor choices when no one is watching can have major effects when people are watching. Our integrity makes an impact.

His Promises

Dear friends, let us continue to love one another, for love comes from God. Anyone who loves is a child of God and knows God. But anyone who does not love does not know God, for God is love.

1 JOHN 4:7-8

The godly walk with integrity;
*   blessed are their children who follow them.*

PROVERBS 20:7

If you are faithful in little things, you will be faithful in large ones. But if you are dishonest in little things, you won't be honest with greater responsibilities.

LUKE 16:10

WE ARE WHAT
WE PRACTICE

Football coaches are notorious for repetition. We show our players game film repeatedly, even if it shows the same situation or play. We outline the same play day after day. Even more than viewing things repeatedly, however, we love to practice them over and over.

The "walk thru" was developed for just this purpose. We talk to our players about what we are going to run, and then we go on the practice field and actually do it—at half speed. No pads, no intensity, just a chance for the players' bodies and brains to perform the action. Later, during practice, we'll do it again, faster and with pads.

The goal is that when game time comes, the players will be ready to simply react without thinking when confronted with situations. They won't have to stop and think through the proper response—it will simply pour out.

In the same way, what we fill ourselves with day in and day out will spill out whether we want it to or not.

The problem comes when we don't allow the Holy Spirit into every area of our lives to help us with the journey and to help us live up to the absolute ideals of God's Word. Help for becoming all we were created to be and power for living up to God's directives for how we should treat others come through the Holy Spirit.

His Promises

Those who are dominated by the sinful nature think about sinful things, but those who are controlled by the Holy Spirit think about things that please the Spirit. So letting your sinful nature control your mind leads to death. But letting the Spirit control your mind leads to life and peace.

ROMANS 8:5-6

The Spirit of the LORD will rest on him—
    the Spirit of wisdom and understanding,
the Spirit of counsel and might,
        the Spirit of knowledge and the fear of the
        LORD.

ISAIAH 11:2

Don't you realize that your body is the temple of the Holy Spirit, who lives in you and was given to you by God? You do not belong to yourself, for God bought you with a high price.

1 CORINTHIANS 6:19-20

YOUR WORD IS
YOUR BOND

"Your word is your bond." My mom said it so often that I can never forget it. My parents were very clear about the importance of character and taught us to choose friends we could trust.

That lesson must have stuck with me, because I have friends of all ages, races, and backgrounds, but I don't hang around people I can't trust. I also hired coaching staffs with that in mind. I always wanted coaches and players who would represent the team well, both on and off the field.

As far as I'm concerned, this is the only way to have a successful team. Ability and talent can't make up for a lack of character. And that applies not only to sports, but to every area of life. In any joint effort—family, work, church, or any other aspect of life—we have to have unwavering trust in each other. I have to be able to depend on you to follow through on what you say, and you have to be able to depend on me to do the same.

We are far more effective in life when we believe it's important to be honest all the time, not just to avoid getting caught in a lie; when we realize winning at all costs isn't worth it when the cost is our integrity; and when we understand that there really is a God who rewards good character.

His Promises

A truthful witness saves lives,
    but a false witness is a traitor.
PROVERBS 14:25

Make them holy by your truth; teach them your word, which is truth.
JOHN 17:17

There are six things the LORD hates—
    no, seven things he detests:
haughty eyes,
    a lying tongue,
    hands that kill the innocent,
a heart that plots evil,

feet that race to do wrong,
a false witness who pours out lies,
a person who sows discord in a family. . . .
Obey your father's commands,
and don't neglect your mother's instruction.

PROVERBS 6:16-20

YOU CAN'T
OUT-GIVE GOD

God says that if we plant sparingly, we will reap sparingly, and if we plant generously, we will reap generously. We should view all that we have—treasure, gifts, abilities, and family—as being things that are God's and on loan to us, His stewards, to use for His glory. When we plant cheerfully, God sees our sincere hearts that believe His plans are good for all our tomorrows and that honor Him when those plans are fulfilled day by day.

Therefore, we should be willing to give back to God all that He has given us, because it is His to begin with. I empathize with pastors who must talk about the financial support of God's church. But we all need to remember that money and other gifts are necessary to expand the Kingdom of God, to reap that generous crop. It's a privilege that should encourage us and give us a sense of boldness because in the end, it is all about God.

If we are about the work of God, God will provide the resources for that work. If we are proclaiming the Word of God with our thoughts, words, and actions, God has the resources to help us do that. When we connect God's mission to change the world with the heart of a cheerful giver who trusts God and understands everything is His, we have the potential for an exponential advancement of His Kingdom.

His Promises

Remember this—a farmer who plants only a few seeds will get a small crop. But the one who plants generously will get a generous crop. You must each decide in your heart how much to give. And don't give reluctantly or in response to pressure. "For God loves a person who gives cheerfully."

2 CORINTHIANS 9:6-7

Give, and you will receive. Your gift will return to you in full—pressed down, shaken together to make room for more, running over, and poured

into your lap. The amount you give will deter-
mine the amount you get back.

LUKE 6:38

Give freely and become more wealthy;
  be stingy and lose everything.
The generous will prosper;
  those who refresh others will themselves
    be refreshed.

PROVERBS 11:24-25

OUT OF THE SPOTLIGHT

Muhammad Ali's signature line was "I am the greatest." He had supreme confidence in his ability, and he knew his attitude sold tickets. His swagger was a novelty.

Today this "look at me" attitude isn't uncommon at all. The more *SportsCenter* moments a player has, the more viewers they will draw and the more valuable they will be to their team—and the more they will be paid. They feel they need to blow their own horns because no one else will. And it seems to work.

But while that attitude gets a lot of attention, it isn't very appealing. Nobody really believes us when we blow our own horns because we're biased. And our focus on ourselves comes across as self-centered and prideful.

Scripture tells us not to praise ourselves but

to let others speak about us. Whatever field we work in, our job is to do the best we can and let our attitude, work ethic, gifts, and skills speak volumes. When we do that, others will eventually notice, and that will mean much more to us and to them than if we had to make them notice with our mouths. God honors humility, not pride.

His Promises

The way you live will always honor and please the Lord, and your lives will produce every kind of good fruit. . . . You will grow as you learn to know God better and better. . . . You will be strengthened with all his glorious power so you will have all the endurance and patience you need.

COLOSSIANS 1:10-11

Anyone who becomes as humble as this little child is the greatest in the Kingdom of Heaven.

MATTHEW 18:4

God opposes the proud
* but gives grace to the humble.*

JAMES 4:6

NO ROOM FOR COMPLAINERS

Let's admit it: All too often, we live in a society of complainers.

Maybe we could put our heads together to figure out how to make the current situation better, something my father always encouraged me to do. The key is to focus on the positives, not the negatives. I agree with Winston Churchill, who said, "For myself I am an optimist—it does not seem to be much use being anything else."

When I was coaching in Tampa Bay, I remember venting at the officials during a game with the New York Giants as we were heading into the locker room—I was totally frustrated at a call they made right at the end of the game. I commented on it afterward to the media.

The next day I apologized to the officials publicly. I knew that people watched me as an example of someone who didn't complain, and I'd totally blown it in that moment when I vented. I felt it only appropriate to apologize to the officials publicly, since my actions were public.

His Promises

Do everything without complaining and arguing, so that no one can criticize you. Live clean, innocent lives as children of God, shining like bright lights in a world full of crooked and perverse people.
PHILIPPIANS 2:14-15

Don't grumble about each other, brothers and sisters, or you will be judged.
JAMES 5:9

Be thankful in all circumstances, for this is God's will for you who belong to Christ Jesus.
1 THESSALONIANS 5:18

LIFE'S
LANDMARKS

Life is full of opportunities to take the easy way.

Temptations are detours from the landmarks that should guide us. Even though we live in a world that considers values to be fluid, subject to change with circumstances or popular opinion, we know we can count on certain absolutes. We all have a sense of right and wrong. Some of us have a lot of practice ignoring that sense, but it's there. And we need to do whatever we can to rely on the landmarks.

If you had parents who instilled good values in you, you have a great foundation. If not, you still know people of integrity who can serve as examples. In either case, we all have access to God's Word, which is the basis for the absolutes we believe and the values we are to live by. These absolutes and values don't change. They aren't a matter of popular opinion. They don't apply to some situations and not to others. They aren't negotiable. We can always count on them to keep us headed in the right direction—even when a more expedient or convenient shortcut tempts us.

His Promises

Hear the instruction of your father,
And do not forsake the law of your mother.

PROVERBS 1:8, NKJV

Humble yourselves before God. Resist the devil, and he will flee from you.

JAMES 4:7

When troubles of any kind come your way, consider it an opportunity for great joy. For you know that when your faith is tested, your endurance has a chance to grow. So let it grow, for when your endurance is fully developed, you will be perfect and complete, needing nothing.

JAMES 1:2-4

PLEASING
THE BOSS

Have you ever thought about how you might approach your job differently if the Lord were your boss?

When I was a player with the Pittsburgh Steelers, we were blessed to have not only men who were great players on our team, but also men with a strong faith in Christ, who tried to do everything to honor and glorify God. To them, He was their ultimate Coach. And things were different within our team as a result.

I wonder what would happen if we began to think that way about our work. I suspect our passion for what we were doing would change drastically if we felt God was in charge.

But wait! God is already our boss! He is the one we ultimately should be answering to each day. He is the one who has given us the gifts, abilities, and talents to use at work, at home, and in other settings. He is the voice of encouragement in our lives. And He offers direction and guidance through His Word and through others. How awesome is that?

His Promises

Work willingly at whatever you do, as though you were working for the Lord rather than for people. Remember that the Lord will give you an inheritance as your reward, and that the Master you are serving is Christ.

COLOSSIANS 3:23-24

Lazy people want much but get little,
    but those who work hard will prosper.

PROVERBS 13:4

May the Lord our God show us his approval
    and make our efforts successful.
    Yes, make our efforts successful!

PSALM 90:17

RICHER
BY THE WORD

When I was coaching, I made a point to have regular Bible studies and chapels for our players and our staff. Game weekends always included a chapel service for which we would have a speaker come in and share a message from Scripture.

Our hope in those settings, as should be the case with any Bible study or prayer group, was to continually plant the empowering and affirming message of Christ in the listeners' hearts and then allow that message to work according to God's purposes in each of them.

How might that look in the various settings of your life? Perhaps at home it starts with prayer in the morning with your spouse and then individual prayer with your children. An encouraging word as your spouse heads out the door to the office or as you drop your children off at school.

Maybe it's getting in the habit of offering an encouraging and kind word to others. Or simply not being a participant in the group gossip session at the watercooler.

Wherever you find yourself, consider ways you can let the word of Christ dwell within you and others.

His Promises

Let the message about Christ, in all its richness, fill your lives. Teach and counsel each other with all the wisdom he gives. Sing psalms and hymns and spiritual songs to God with thankful hearts. And whatever you do or say, do it as a representative of the Lord Jesus, giving thanks through him to God the Father.

COLOSSIANS 3:16-17

Where two or three gather together as my followers, I am there among them.

MATTHEW 18:20

Rejoice in our confident hope. Be patient in trouble, and keep on praying.

ROMANS 12:12

CONFIDENCE
VS.
PRIDE

Barry Sanders and Deion Sanders both worked hard and were considered good teammates. But their public personas were very different. Deion was known as "Prime Time"—flashy, loud, and proud.

Barry was just the opposite. When he scored a touchdown, he handed the ball to the official and went back to the bench. In postgame interviews, he would praise the linemen who blocked for him.

Both players got a lot of attention for their accomplishments, but Deion got even more for his showmanship. Deion still commands the spotlight, but these days, it's mostly to talk about the Lord.

Confidence is a good quality to have. It's a realization that God has given us certain abilities and created us to fulfill a unique role that no one else can fill. It's a humble recognition that life is not about us but about using our gifts and abilities to their fullest to help others and contribute to society. Pride, on the other hand, is all about building ourselves up in the eyes of others. If we want to keep from falling, we need to learn the difference.

His Promises

Pride goes before destruction,
and haughtiness before a fall.
PROVERBS 16:18

It is not that we think we are qualified to do anything on our own. Our qualification comes from God.
2 CORINTHIANS 3:5

I can do nothing on my own. I judge as God tells me. Therefore, my judgment is just, because I carry out the will of the one who sent me, not my own will.
JOHN 5:30

RIGHT, OR JUST CONVENIENT?

Every day brings a series of decisions between doing what's convenient and what's right. And those choices often carry longer-term consequences than we realize. The difference between "convenient" and "right" can last a lifetime.

Integrity is what you do when no one is watching. It's doing the right thing all the time, even when it works to your disadvantage. It's the internal compass that keeps you pointed in the right direction when there are plenty of other options around and many of them are pulling you away from your purpose.

When you have integrity, people can count on you. A teammate with integrity can be trusted to put in the time to prepare, to learn the game plan, and to know his assignments during the game. A business partner with integrity can be counted on to deal with money honestly and with people respectfully. A marriage partner with integrity can be trusted to be faithful and to be "all in" for better and for worse, not just for better. A friend with integrity can be depended on to keep his word and to stick with you through thick and thin.

Integrity touches every area of life, not just now but in the long run. And it can sometimes seem like a rare commodity. But the choices of a person with integrity become a blessing not only to that person but to everyone he or she relates to.

His Promises

Who may worship in your sanctuary, LORD?
Who may enter your presence on your
holy hill? . . .
Those who despise flagrant sinners,
and honor the faithful followers of the LORD,
and keep their promises even when it hurts.

PSALM 15:1, 4

The LORD is more pleased when we do what is
      right and just
  than when we offer him sacrifices.

PROVERBS 21:3

Pray for us, for our conscience is clear and we
want to live honorably in everything we do.

HEBREWS 13:18

QUIET STRENGTH

Some people wear their status on their sleeves. And if you can't tell by looking, they will let you know by dropping a few names of people they associate with.

Other people have the same status, but you wouldn't know it from the way they look or talk. They may have obvious leadership skills, but they don't have the self-promoting attitude to go with it. They know how to make others feel significant.

True humility focuses on building others up. It's embracing the idea that God created each one for a particular place and time, and it's being completely comfortable viewing others with exactly the same significance. When someone can do that, it becomes much easier to let go of status or an unhealthy need for respect.

The best way to earn respect is to respect others simply because they are who they are. Those who have that attitude make the best spouses, family members, teammates, friends, and business partners. Humility earns the respect that pride seeks.

His Promises

The LORD mocks the mockers
but is gracious to the humble.
PROVERBS 3:34

Let us think of ways to motivate one another
to acts of love and good works.
HEBREWS 10:24

The LORD has told you what is good,
and this is what he requires of you:
to do what is right, to love mercy,
and to walk humbly with your God.
MICAH 6:8

RELAX, GOD'S GOT YOUR BACK

All of us have been affected at some point along the way by the thoughtless words and hurtful actions of others. And no matter how much we have heard about God's love for us, we sometimes struggle to believe that we can actually experience that kind of love.

Whether you realize it or not, God has created you with unique gifts and abilities, called you to a fulfilling purpose, and plans to use you for extraordinary accomplishments. Maybe there seem to be too many obstacles to get over—or you're in a situation that seems to have no way out or room for growth. Or maybe you think you've made too many mistakes. But God isn't limited by these things, and neither are you. The God who created you is still there and loves you with an unending love.

what God has put us here to do and then doing it as well and as faithfully as we can. When our hearts and our actions are true to our callings, God considers us successful. And in the end, His is the only scoreboard that counts.

His Promises

This Book of the Law shall not depart from your mouth, but you shall meditate in it day and night, that you may observe to do according to all that is written in it. For then you will make your way prosperous, and then you will have good success.

JOSHUA 1:8, NKJV

Submit to God, and you will have peace; then things will go well for you.

JOB 22:21

We are God's masterpiece. He has created us anew in Christ Jesus, so we can do the good things he planned for us long ago.

EPHESIANS 2:10

WHAT TRUE LOVE LOOKS LIKE

Let's face it, good examples of true, sacrificial love that builds others up are hard to find.

According to 1 Corinthians 13, love means doing everything for someone else's benefit. That doesn't mean passively giving in to the other person's every wish or desire, and it obviously doesn't mean dominating a relationship. It means making every decision with the other person's well-being in mind. Whether in marriage, in other family relationships, or among friends, the principle is the same: Love seeks to strengthen and benefit others.

Be active in the lives of others. Talk to them and, more important, listen to them. Invest your time and your attention. Be supportive and be involved. Real love changes lives—including yours.

His Promises

Love never gives up, never loses faith, is always hopeful, and endures through every circumstance.

1 CORINTHIANS 13:7

Above all, clothe yourselves with love, which binds us all together in perfect harmony.

COLOSSIANS 3:14

There is no greater love than to lay down one's life for one's friends.

JOHN 15:13

JUST DEAL WITH IT

When conflict arises, it can get awfully tempting to simply brush it aside to "deal with it later," especially if it's something you've dealt with before.

Let me urge you not to do that. Don't let the sun go down on your anger. Find a moment to let the emotion pass, and even if it can't all be resolved then, try to find a way to take the edge off the moment. Find common ground. Agree to come back to it later. But don't stay angry and put it off until another time.

Believe it or not, conflict isn't always bad. It's a way of identifying the differences we have. We all have conflict in our lives—it's how we deal with the situations that make the difference. Will we be charitable and understanding? Or harsh and hardened? The choice is ours.

Every day presents opportunities to practice patience, understanding, and compromise. Talk things out and don't force your opinion. Listen to each other instead of resorting to the silent treatment.

Above all else, be wise. Don't provoke, and don't brush things aside.

His Promises

"Don't sin by letting anger control you." Don't let the sun go down while you are still angry, for anger gives a foothold to the devil.
EPHESIANS 4:26-27

If another believer sins against you, go privately and point out the offense. If the other person listens and confesses it, you have won that person back.
MATTHEW 18:15

God blesses those who work for peace, for they will be called the children of God.
MATTHEW 5:9

TOUGH LOVE

It must have been a tough assignment to go from being the Son of God on His Father's right hand to being a regular guy on earth.

Jesus had to endure beatings, scourging, a crown of thorns, spittle, cursing, and then being hanged on a cross.

The truth is that we would have been eternally lost if He had not done all of that.

God's plan was to save His people, and the only way God could eternally pardon us was through His Son—Jesus Christ.

Jesus became a flesh-and-blood man, a human being with desires and passions similar to ours, except for one difference: He was without sin. In His humanity He identified with us, but more than that, we identified with Him. And that drew us closer to Him—a blessed place to be.

His Promises

When we were utterly helpless, Christ came at just the right time and died for us sinners. Now, most people would not be willing to die for an upright person, though someone might perhaps be willing to die for a person who is especially good. But God showed his great love for us by sending Christ to die for us while we were still sinners.

ROMANS 5:6-8

You, O Lord,
*   are a God of compassion and mercy,*
slow to get angry
*   and filled with unfailing love and*
*   faithfulness.*

PSALM 86:15

The LORD must wait for you to come to him
*   so he can show you his love and compassion.*
For the LORD is a faithful God.
*   Blessed are those who wait for his help.*

ISAIAH 30:18

WHAT FATHERS SHOULD KNOW BEST

I worry about the vacuum left in our culture by absentee fathers. I know the obstacles can be enormous; a lot of men are divorced or have jobs that keep them on the road much of the time. It's hard to balance meeting the family's financial needs with meeting their emotional needs.

And even when a man is in the home, he can become an "absentee father" by turning his kids over to the TV set or video games, or to other people. The children often get the leftovers of Dad's time.

Those of us who are fathers need to be careful to not become absentee dads—at any level, whether by being away from home too much or by being unavailable when we're there. Too many kids, especially young men and boys, are growing up without a male role model in the house. Our society often equates fatherhood with financial support, but it's so much more.

There is no better way to make a mark in this world, to shape the next generation, and to leave a lasting legacy than to show love and acceptance to your own kids.

His Promises

Fathers, do not aggravate your children, or they will become discouraged.

COLOSSIANS 3:21

Direct your children onto the right path,
and when they are older, they will not
leave it.

PROVERBS 22:6

The LORD is like a father to his children,
tender and compassionate to those who
fear him.

PSALM 103:13

"I SPY" BLESSINGS ALL AROUND ME

It's another day. As important as your schedule may be, take time to look around and acknowledge your blessings. They are all around you, and every day is the perfect time to celebrate them. Why? Because He created them especially for you.

They're in the hope-filled sunrise filtering through our windows, the wrinkled red face of a newborn baby, a grandmother's gentle smile, or the trusting laugh of a child.

We find the blessings of God in a table full of food and in those members of the family we share it with. In the opportunity to watch our sons' baseball games or to love our adult children, because we missed the opportunities to fully love them as they grew. Maybe we get the "second chance" in the blessing of our grand-children, to love them no-holds-barred.

Speaking of kids: Their sense of awe and wonder has to make God smile. They can rattle off big and small things that can be considered a blessing from God, like dolphins unexpectedly breaking the surface of the bay, or the twinkle of stars millions of miles away, right where we left them the night before. Take a cue from them, and you'll come up with an endless list.

No matter what you may be facing right now, take a few minutes, look around at all that God has created, thank Him, and savor the gift. Don't get so wrapped up in today's worries or tomorrow's "urgent" priorities that you miss the beautiful things right in front of you.

His Promises

All praise to God, the Father of our Lord Jesus Christ, who has blessed us with every spiritual blessing in the heavenly realms because we are united with Christ.

EPHESIANS 1:3

Whatever is good and perfect is a gift coming down to us from God our Father, who created all the lights in the heavens. He never changes or casts a shifting shadow.

JAMES 1:17

Ask, using my name, and you will receive, and you will have abundant joy.

JOHN 16:24

A CURE FOR LOW SELF-ESTEEM

So much of what we do as human beings—so many of the mistakes we make and desires we have—flows from having very little self-esteem. Many of us wear masks, strive for unworthy goals, get into bad relationships, compromise our integrity, or just blend in with the crowd because deep down inside we're wounded and needy.

But remember this: You were created by God. Before you were ever born, He knew who you would be. You are designed with a unique combination of abilities, interests, and passions that has never been before and will never be seen in anyone again.

Not only that, you are created for eternal impact. Your one-of-a-kind design was intended to last. He guards over your purpose and destiny, He is aware of all your needs, and He watches you even while you sleep. You are an intentional part of His plan. You are family, and He is your Father; He designed you for incredible purposes.

If that sinks into your heart—really becomes a part of who you are at your core—you will never have problems with low self-esteem. Your heart and mind will be filled with a healthy sense of self-worth that enables you to know your purpose in life and to fulfill it.

His Promises

You made all the delicate, inner parts of my body
and knit me together in my mother's
womb. . . .
You saw me before I was born.
Every day of my life was recorded in your book.
Every moment was laid out
before a single day had passed.

PSALM 139:13, 16

Each time he said, "My grace is all you need.
My power works best in weakness." So now I am
glad to boast about my weaknesses, so that the
power of Christ can work through me.

2 CORINTHIANS 12:9

You are a chosen people. You are royal priests, a holy nation, God's very own possession. As a result, you can show others the goodness of God, for he called you out of the darkness into his wonderful light.

1 PETER 2:9

IN IT FOR THE LONG HAUL

Every year, football fans expect their teams to win. And if the previous season ended with a poor record, they want to see a change.

However, the best moves that teams make are often done without changing personnel. Sometimes the biggest improvement in productivity comes from players who are already on your roster, who have had a year to mature and grow, to learn your team's system and become further acclimated in their roles and responsibilities. Those teams never end up being the fan darlings in June or July, however, because they haven't "done enough to improve."

We're all like that. We think the grass is greener elsewhere, that the big splash is the best way to reach our goals. But sometimes the employees you already have will be the best fit for that new position in your organization. Give them a chance to prove themselves.

So next spring when the flowers bloom and the free agents switch teams, don't lose faith if not many names change on your team's roster. Sometimes the teams that focus on growing with the same personnel are the ones that make the greatest improvement and achieve lasting success.

His Promises

Let's not get tired of doing what is good. At just the right time we will reap a harvest of blessing if we don't give up.
GALATIANS 6:9

If we look forward to something we don't yet have, we must wait patiently and confidently.
ROMANS 8:25

Be still in the presence of the LORD,
    and wait patiently for him to act.
PSALM 37:7

LISTEN UP

When preparing my team for a game, I often used a lot of different ways to get my message across. I would show a video of our upcoming opponent or have the assistant coaches go over scouting reports on that team's strengths and weaknesses. We would pass out diagrams of plays we intended to run or defenses we would use that week. Sometimes I would have a guest speaker or veteran player address the team about the importance of playing well that week. Many different people and materials, but all delivering the message that I wanted to get across.

The same is true with God. God has been speaking to us since the beginning of Creation. He is always speaking to us, despite the fact that more often than not, we are not listening. Sometimes we're waiting to hear that big booming voice of God, but that's not how He speaks. Instead, He speaks to us in the quiet words of our spouse, a parent, one of our children, or a friend.

God knows what He is saying and how to say it—we need to be still and listen for His voice.

His Promises

Show me the right path, O LORD;
    point out the road for me to follow.
Lead me by your truth and teach me,
    for you are the God who saves me.
    All day long I put my hope in you.

PSALM 25:4-5

Look! I stand at the door and knock. If you hear my voice and open the door, I will come in.

REVELATION 3:20

Trust in the LORD with all your heart;
    do not depend on your own understanding.
Seek his will in all you do,
    and he will show you which path to take.

PROVERBS 3:5-6

CALM BEFORE
THE STORM

When we're in the middle of tough situations, we tend to worry, which does little to help us overcome the problem. In fact, it usually makes things worse.

In the midst of those storms we shouldn't be worrying, we should be praying, a discipline recommended by none other than Jesus Christ. And at the very outset of prayer, it will bring us to a place of peace.

Throughout Scripture, God makes it abundantly clear to us that we are to pray, to devote ourselves to prayer, to pray without ceasing, to pray continually, and to pray boldly with the God who loves us. Jesus prayed continually to His Father. In fact, he "often withdrew to the wilderness for prayer" (Luke 5:16).

So why don't we pray as consistently and

fervently as we should to our Father? Maybe we don't believe anything will happen, or that our prayers won't result in the answers we seek. Maybe it's not a habit we have developed, and therefore when the opportunity arises for a time of prayer, it is not a default for us.

The next time something occurs, and you sense worry taking over, turn whatever you're going through to a sense of peace by praying— you'll be pleasantly surprised.

His Promises

In times of trouble, may the LORD answer
>*your cry.*
>>*May the name of the God of Jacob keep you*
>>>*safe from all harm. . . .*
May we shout for joy when we hear of your
>*victory*
>>*and raise a victory banner in the name*
>>>*of our God.*
May the LORD answer all your prayers.

PSALM 20:1, 5

When you pray, go away by yourself, shut the door behind you, and pray to your Father in private. Then your Father, who sees everything, will reward you.

MATTHEW 6:6

Ask me and I will tell you remarkable secrets you do not know about things to come.

JEREMIAH 33:3

MVP (MANY VALUABLE PEOPLE)

Since the first Super Bowl in 1967 through Super Bowl LIV in 2020, fifty-five Most Valuable Player awards have been handed out.

The breakdown by position of the Most Valuable Player selected is kick returner—1; running backs—7; wide receivers—7; defensive players—10; quarterbacks—30.

In the history of the Super Bowl, not one offensive lineman has won the award. Yet try to play the game without them. Try to win a Super Bowl without a stellar offensive line. And as to quarterbacks—how many Super Bowl MVP awards do you think they would have won if they had been consistently hurried, hit, or sacked during a game, watching the game from the vantage point of their backsides?

Many parts—one team, one body. All together.

His Promises

Just as our bodies have many parts and each part has a special function, so it is with Christ's body. We are many parts of one body, and we all belong to each other.

ROMANS 12:4-5

He makes the whole body fit together perfectly. As each part does its own special work, it helps the other parts grow, so that the whole body is healthy and growing and full of love.

EPHESIANS 4:16

Two people are better off than one, for they can help each other succeed. If one person falls, the other can reach out and help. But someone who falls alone is in real trouble.

ECCLESIASTES 4:9-10

EDGING OFF
THE PATH

Sometimes we act as if it's the large things that trip us up—as if we merely need to avoid big pitfalls. But it's actually the small things that so often make us stumble.

Joe Marciano, an assistant coach for me in Tampa, had a saying that always resonated with our team: "Death by inches." When a team is winning, coaches have a tendency to let little details slide by because things are going well. Then suddenly we're in a losing streak and can't figure out why. It's because those small, infrequent mistakes that didn't get corrected have become the norm, and the team can't get that sharpness back.

It can happen in life as well. We know the rules to keep ourselves out of trouble. But then there's one compromise. Then another. Before we know it, we're so far off course, we can't imagine how we got there. Of course, looking back, we can trace the path: one small step at a time.

We know that the life God calls us to is straight ahead. Be aware and wary of the small things that can lead you off track.

His Promises

Don't do as the wicked do,
and don't follow the path of evildoers.
Don't even think about it; don't go that way.
Turn away and keep moving.

PROVERBS 4:14-15

You can enter God's Kingdom only through
the narrow gate. The highway to hell is broad,
and its gate is wide for the many who choose
that way.

MATTHEW 7:13

Your word is a lamp to guide my feet
and a light for my path.

PSALM 119:105

REACH OUT AND TOUCH SOMEONE

Communication is easier now than it has ever been. But have you thought about what we may be losing when we depend more on electronic contact and less on face-to-face communication? Our deepest, most meaningful relationships develop in one-on-one time and extended conversation. We can read facial expressions, pick up on emotional responses, and communicate our own feelings very clearly. The result is more interaction, more depth, and more substance.

I believe that if Jesus had all the communication tools of today at His disposal, He would still choose to spend His time face-to-face with His disciples. He would still heal people by touching them physically and be close enough to them that when He spoke to them they could hear the compassion in His voice. God designed relationships to be developed and strengthened through personal, face-to-face interaction.

The communication tools available to us today are wonderful. But when we start to depend on technology as a substitute for one-on-one time with each other, we are missing an important key to relationships. We need to make sure we're not so connected with everything out there that we miss the chance to connect with the people directly in front of us.

His Promises

Be happy with those who are happy, and weep with those who weep.
ROMANS 12:15

This is my commandment: Love each other in the same way I have loved you.
JOHN 15:12

God called you to do good, even if it means suffering, just as Christ suffered for you. He is your example, and you must follow in his steps.
1 PETER 2:21

FAITH THAT
DISPELS DOUBT

Doubt always seems to stick its destructive head into all we are trying to do. That's where faith comes in. Faith isn't the absence of doubt, but it reaches beyond doubt and toward that which we believe to be true. Or as the writer of Hebrews puts it, "Faith shows the reality of what we hope for; it is the evidence of things we cannot see" (11:1).

On the football field, I'm sure our guys had occasional moments of doubt before the game got started. But we had to push that aside and replace our doubts with information we knew to be true. When we created a vision of what the desired outcome would look like and focused on those things that we knew we could accomplish, there was little room left for doubt.

I like the story of the perpetual optimist. He

fell off the roof of a ten-story building and still had a smile on his face when he passed the fifth floor on the way down. When someone yelled out the window, "How are you?" he answered, "Okay so far!" That may seem to be an unrealistic faith that flies in the face of scientific knowledge— gravity. But it's still faith. Many of us don't know how a plane takes off, stays in the air, and lands, yet we step on the plane in faith that it will fly.

Doesn't it make even more sense to believe the promises of the Creator of the universe, whose work is visible all around us?

His Promises

"What do you mean, 'If I can'?" Jesus asked. "Anything is possible if a person believes."

MARK 9:23

Have you never heard?
    Have you never understood?
The LORD is the everlasting God,
    the Creator of all the earth.
He never grows weak or weary.
    No one can measure the depths of his
      understanding.

ISAIAH 40:28

All praise to God, the Father of our Lord Jesus Christ. It is by his great mercy that we have been born again, because God raised Jesus Christ from the dead. Now we live with great expectation, and we have a priceless inheritance—an inheritance that is kept in heaven for you, pure and undefiled, beyond the reach of change and decay.

1 PETER 1:3-4

BE KIND

It's easy to get caught up in an attempt to prove we're right and someone else is completely wrong. But when others disagree with you, do you automatically put up walls or do you try to find common ground for discussion?

When we dig in and become immovable in our views, even belittling another person's belief in order to win the argument, we are undermining Christ's Kingdom.

Conflict is unavoidable, but combat is a choice. Conflict can illuminate differences, and in the process, actually help us. But pushing it to the next level of combat is rarely, if ever, productive.

And sometimes it seems like our response is more strident if it's a Christian who takes a position contrary to ours. Or if the church takes a position we believe to be wrong. Rather than striving for peace, we automatically wage war, moving into combat before we have provided an opportunity to understand the differences.

God wants us to bring people together, to build bridges, not walls, wherever possible. Especially within His church.

His Promises

God blesses those who work for peace,
*   for they will be called the children of God.*
MATTHEW 5:9

Your kindness will reward you,
*   but your cruelty will destroy you.*
PROVERBS 11:17

Understand this, my dear brothers and sisters:
You must all be quick to listen, slow to speak,
and slow to get angry.
JAMES 1:19

THE REWARDS
OF PATIENCE

In our world of constant connectivity, instant gratification, and immediate results, patience seems in short supply.

There were times when we had to quickly fill holes on our team created by free agency or retirement or injury. However, our preference was always to approach these needs patiently, thoughtfully, and corporately with as much input as possible.

Even though in the NFL there is the ever-present pressure to win the Super Bowl, we found that our slow, careful method was a better way to build for the future. It provided a longer-term satisfaction and joy within our organization. And since everyone had an opportunity to contribute in some way, they claimed ownership in the decisions and direction we undertook.

How well do you score on the patience scale? When you make one snap decision after another, it could affect your health, your family, and even your job or business. If possible, take time and seek additional input from others before something is set in stone. From my experience, I believe a person always benefits from different perspectives.

His Promises

Be patient with everyone.
1 THESSALONIANS 5:14

We can rejoice, too, when we run into problems and trials, for we know that they help us develop endurance. And endurance develops strength of character, and character strengthens our confident hope of salvation. And this hope will not lead to disappointment. For we know how dearly God loves us, because he has given us the Holy Spirit to fill our hearts with his love.
ROMANS 5:3-5

Finishing is better than starting.
Patience is better than pride.
ECCLESIASTES 7:8

SOUND ADVICE IN A NOISY WORLD

No matter how many friends you have, you probably only turn to a few when you need advice. But most of us let a few other voices affect us too. The opinion of the crowd sometimes weighs more than it should. There's no shortage of internal voices either: ambition, power, wealth, revenge, greed, pleasure, compromise, and self-centeredness. In one respect or another, all of these voices—whether internal or external—are simply expressing the ways of the world.

Learn to tune in to the quiet voices that consistently speak truth to you. First and foremost, that's God. Practice hearing His gentle whisper. But also listen to the counsel of those you trust: your spouse, your parents and other family members, your close friends. These people know you well, they have been with you in the valleys and on the mountaintops, and unlike many other voices, they want what's best for you.

His Promises

Only simpletons believe everything they're told!
The prudent carefully consider their steps.

PROVERBS 14:15

My child, listen to what I say,
and treasure my commands.
Tune your ears to wisdom,
and concentrate on understanding.
Cry out for insight,
and ask for understanding.
Search for them as you would for silver;
seek them like hidden treasures.
Then you will understand what it means to fear
the LORD,
and you will gain knowledge of God.

PROVERBS 2:1-5

Pay close attention to what you hear. The closer
you listen, the more understanding you will be
given—and you will receive even more.

MARK 4:24

LONELY AT
THE BOTTOM

We have all heard the term "down and out." Churches and other ministries develop programs to reach folks down on their luck: soup kitchens, homeless shelters, community food and clothing ministries, housing assistance.

Getting up close and personal with someone who is genuinely struggling may turn into a friendship or it may not. But it's certainly worth a try.

We should all strive to stay connected to the good things around us—our family and friends who have been with us throughout our journey—and seek to add other friends who will have a positive impact on us. In addition, we need to be proactive in seeking out and encouraging others, helping to keep them from becoming disconnected themselves.

Don't ever assume that someone doesn't need an encouraging word or your friendship, no matter what that person's status might be.

His Promises

Brothers and sisters, we urge you to warn those who are lazy. Encourage those who are timid. Take tender care of those who are weak. Be patient with everyone.
1 THESSALONIANS 5:14

Your love for one another will prove to the world that you are my disciples.
JOHN 13:35

Accept other believers who are weak in faith, and don't argue with them about what they think is right or wrong.
ROMANS 14:1

THE GREATEST COMMANDMENT

We've all seen people less fortunate than ourselves, people who seem to have little hope for change unless someone intervenes. We've seen communities and nations go through difficulties and wrestle with problems like starvation or disease that we may never have to worry about. We may not have a full solution to any of these problems, but we can affect lives one at a time.

Our purpose is to serve God and use whatever He has given us to help others. When we focus on that, we find the joy and abundant life Jesus promised. We find that we are much more fulfilled when we use our passions and abilities to make a difference in someone's life.

You may not reach every goal in life—in fact, you probably won't—but you can fulfill your purpose. When you love God, you are doing what He made you for; and when you love others, you are expressing His own attitude toward them. You can find peace and happiness in the knowledge that you are satisfying your purpose and honoring Him.

His Promises

"'You must love the LORD your God with all your heart, all your soul, all your strength, and all your mind.' And, 'Love your neighbor as yourself.'" . . . "Do this and you will live!"

LUKE 10:27-28

Work willingly at whatever you do, as though you were working for the Lord rather than for people. Remember that the Lord will give you an inheritance as your reward, and that the Master you are serving is Christ.

COLOSSIANS 3:23-24

Even the Son of Man came not to be served but to serve others and to give his life as a ransom for many.

MARK 10:45

HOLD YOUR GROUND

It's easy to waver in the face of temptation.

We can be cruising along at times in life, doing what God has set before us . . . then *things* show up that distract us, dishearten us, and tempt us to stray.

Stay rooted to people who are of similar mind and have a similar focus on God and Christ.

Similarly, stay grounded in and connected to your family. Everyone gets busy, and it's easy to get disconnected a little bit at a time. Don't let it happen.

Finally, make sure that you stay tethered tightly to God through regular personal quiet time and fellowship with others through reading the Bible, prayer, and worship.

God, through the leading of the Holy Spirit

within us, is unwavering and always absolutely right in where He leads us.

His Promises

If you think you are standing strong, be careful not to fall. The temptations in your life are no different from what others experience. And God is faithful. He will not allow the temptation to be more than you can stand. When you are tempted, he will show you a way out so that you can endure.

1 CORINTHIANS 10:12-13

Keep watch and pray, so that you will not give in to temptation. For the spirit is willing, but the body is weak!

MATTHEW 26:41

Put on all of God's armor so that you will be able to stand firm against all strategies of the devil.

EPHESIANS 6:11

WILLING TO STAND ALONE

It's hard to stand alone against popular opinion. We feel pressure to compromise, and it's easy at such times to lose perspective on what's important to cling to and what isn't. Sometimes we realize we were wrong about something, sometimes we still believe we're right but it isn't worth fighting for, and sometimes we stand firm on what we know is true and worth fighting for. But knowing the difference can be difficult.

As a Christian, you need to be stubborn about the things God says are right. Always stand firm on essentials. Focus on the main thing, the truths that are most important and worth fighting for. Be single-minded about pursuing Christ, His Kingdom, and the things that are important to Him, and be persistent. Sometimes we have to stand alone for a long time. But be willing to compromise on non-essentials. Let go of what isn't important and be comfortable admitting when you're wrong. Your convictions combined with your humility may even attract others to your viewpoint, and you won't be standing alone for long.

His Promises

I focus on this one thing: Forgetting the past and looking forward to what lies ahead, I press on to reach the end of the race and receive the heavenly prize for which God, through Christ Jesus, is calling us.

PHILIPPIANS 3:13-14

Remember, it is sin to know what you ought to do and then not do it.

JAMES 4:17

Don't team up with those who are unbelievers. How can righteousness be a partner with wickedness? How can light live with darkness?

2 CORINTHIANS 6:14

KICKERS
KNOW BEST

During my career as a player and a coach, I worked with some of the best kickers in the National Football League, and one thing they all had in common was the ability to focus on the positive. They always believed they were going to make the next kick, because they knew from experience that negative thoughts would doom their efforts.

Essentially, these kickers do what the apostle Paul suggests we do in whatever setting we find ourselves: focus on the positive; fix our thoughts on things that are good and right and pure. On the field or in our homes or at work, when we think of our spouses, our children, friends, employees, or coworkers—we should fix our thoughts on what is true, and honorable, and right, and pure, and lovely, and admirable.

We should think about things that are excellent and worthy of praise.

Adopting a positive attitude, even when you're under pressure or the odds seem stacked against you, nearly always assures a positive outcome.

His Promises

Fix your thoughts on what is true, and honorable, and right, and pure, and lovely, and admirable. Think about things that are excellent and worthy of praise.

PHILIPPIANS 4:8

Therefore, since we have been made right in God's sight by faith, we have peace with God because of what Jesus Christ our Lord has done for us. Because of our faith, Christ has brought us into this place of undeserved privilege where we now stand, and we confidently and joyfully look forward to sharing God's glory.

ROMANS 5:1-2

Jesus Christ is the same yesterday, today, and forever.

HEBREWS 13:8

FREE TO DISAGREE

During football games, we have an unwritten code that if you're on the headsets, whether in the coaches' box or on the sideline, it's a safe place and you are free to say whatever you want to say. We can disagree with one another, float crazy ideas, and change our minds without recrimination. It's not a time for idle chatter, of course, but it's a circumstance where people can speak their minds without fear of insult or of someone holding a grudge against them the next day. We don't always agree—and that's a good thing—but the conversation will be healthy and helpful because different people analyze situations differently. You have your opinion, I have mine, and neither of us will hold it against the other person.

When you disagree with a coworker or

friend or spouse or pastor, how do you handle it? With grace and understanding or with anger and bitterness? The productivity and harmony of your workplace or home will be directly affected by your response. And your witness may be impacted too; others may see you or Jesus in a different light if you can't handle conflict.

His Promises

Don't get involved in foolish, ignorant arguments that only start fights. A servant of the Lord must not quarrel but must be kind to everyone, be able to teach, and be patient with difficult people.

2 TIMOTHY 2:23-24

Be obedient, always ready to do what is good. [You] must not slander anyone and must avoid quarreling. Instead, [you] should be gentle and show true humility to everyone.

TITUS 3:1-2

So then, let us aim for harmony in the church and try to build each other up.

ROMANS 14:19

TIPS FOR A HEALTHY HEART

The Bible emphasizes the importance of guarding our hearts. That's because our hearts can determine the course of our lives. Our thoughts, emotions, and intentions will shape everything we do and every decision we make. So it's vitally important for us and those close to us to guard our inner attitudes. Here are some ways to do that.

First, be careful what you take in. Just as your physical health is affected by what you eat, your spiritual and emotional health is affected by the thoughts and images you consume. Avoid spiritual "junk food" and fill your heart with positive messages.

Second, fill yourself with God's Word. Nothing will influence you as powerfully as hearing God's voice and learning His ways. Read His Word and meditate on it often.

Third, stay grounded in prayer. Just remember that prayer is simply having a conversation with God. There are no rules or special words. Just talk to Him openly and honestly.

Finally, check your motives for what you do with God and for Him. Make sure everything you do—especially what you do in your relationship with God—is done out of a sincere desire to know God, discover His will, and do it.

Pay attention to what goes in, and you'll be pleased with what comes out.

His Promises

Guard your heart above all else,
for it determines the course of your life.

PROVERBS 4:23

All Scripture is inspired by God and is useful
to teach us what is true and to make us realize
what is wrong in our lives. It corrects us when
we are wrong and teaches us to do what is right.
God uses it to prepare and equip his people to do
every good work.

2 TIMOTHY 3:16-17

I have hidden your word in my heart,
that I might not sin against you.

PSALM 119:11

REACHING INCREMENTAL GOALS

Few of us want to remain where we are without any improvement or increase. God has wired us to want to grow. But what kind of growth are we looking for?

Sometimes our goals are a steady step-by-step progression, and sometimes they require risk. Whenever we ask God to enlarge our territories, we need faith to move to the next level. That always comes with the possibility of failure, although we can trust Him to be with us either to help us get there or to catch us when we fall. Over time, those steps of faith pay off. We grow and improve and reach higher goals.

Remember to focus on goals that are within your control. As a coach, I worked on learning more and improving my coaching abilities in order to be qualified for positions with greater responsibility. I couldn't control whether I would be hired for those positions. When you do your part to prepare, you can trust God for the results. In His timing, He's the one who enlarges your territory. Your job is to make yourself ready for it.

His Promises

Look straight ahead,
and fix your eyes on what lies before you.
PROVERBS 4:25

Because the Sovereign LORD helps me,
I will not be disgraced.
Therefore, I have set my face like a stone,
determined to do his will.
And I know that I will not be put to shame.
ISAIAH 50:7

We ask God to give you complete knowledge of
his will and to give you spiritual wisdom and
understanding.
COLOSSIANS 1:9

THE FUN OF FAITH

There are times where it would be nice to know the answer before the question comes to mind. To know the result before you try something. To know the outcome before you start.

But then where's the fun and challenge in that?

We may not know what awaits us around the next bend, but we need to the have the faith to know that God is not only with us before we get to the bend, but that he will be with us around that next bend as well—and the one after that, and the one after that.

It is all part and parcel of finishing the work that God gave us to tell the world about the Good News and the wonderful love of God.

Life is full of uncertainty; God wants you to be bolstered by faith in Him.

His Promises

Faith shows the reality of what we hope for; it is the evidence of things we cannot see.

HEBREWS 11:1

It is impossible to please God without faith. Anyone who wants to come to him must believe that God exists and that he rewards those who sincerely seek him.

HEBREWS 11:6

O my people, trust in him at all times.
Pour out your heart to him,
for God is our refuge.

PSALM 62:8

A COUPLE OF
MINUTES A DAY

Do you have moments in your life when you feel like everyone is demanding a piece of you, looking for you everywhere, armed with all their urgent requests and deadlines?

The Gospels mention some similar moments for Jesus—times when He realized it was time for Him to get away to be by Himself.

But this idea of stopping what we're doing and getting alone with the Father? For most of us it's not part of our DNA. It is certainly not embraced by society. They would most likely label us as recluses or as displaying antisocial behavior. Instead of pulling away, taking some time, getting some rest—society says to charge on, full speed ahead.

Find some moments of your day—perhaps

in the morning—to spend time alone with God.

God wants there to be times when you simply escape with Him, alone, and recharge. Like you are doing right now, reading this. He wants to be with you and help you to slow down for a few moments and seek Him. It will give the two of you the chance you need to hang out together.

His Promises

Let all that I am wait quietly before God,
*   for my hope is in him.*
PSALM 62:5

It is good to wait quietly
*   for salvation from the LORD.*
LAMENTATIONS 3:26

Only in returning to me
*   and resting in me will you be saved.*
In quietness and confidence is your strength.
ISAIAH 30:15

ENERGIZED BY FAILURE

Thomas Edison made many attempts at inventing a working light bulb with setback after setback. Yet he was confident he hadn't failed even once. He had simply found ten thousand ways not to make a light bulb. That's a great perspective when you face adversity. In the effort toward any worthwhile goal, failure has to be considered part of the process. Failure in achieving a particular result isn't really failure if it's another step on the way toward the goal. It can be a vital part of the journey.

Don't get discouraged when you fail. In fact, consider it a normal part of learning. Though many people treat it as a dirty little secret and wear masks to cover it up, successful people have learned to be comfortable trying something that doesn't work out. Success isn't about never failing; it's about persevering through mistakes and adversity. If you persist, even your failures can turn into a valuable part of your success story.

His Promises

My health may fail, and my spirit may grow weak,
> *but God remains the strength of my heart;*
> *he is mine forever.*

PSALM 73:26

The godly may trip seven times, but they will get up again.
> *But one disaster is enough to overthrow the wicked.*

PROVERBS 24:16

Be strong and immovable. Always work enthusi-astically for the Lord, for you know that nothing you do for the Lord is ever useless.

1 CORINTHIANS 15:58

GET YOUR
EYES CHECKED

Our vision is influenced by how we see the world. Do we see it through the lens of the hope and joy that our faith in Christ brings? Do we see it through the lens that knows we'll be in heaven for eternity, that our potential in God's hands is unlimited, and that the challenges of the moment are but a blink of an eye in eternity? Or do we see the world through a lens of fear and despair and see our potential as limited? I pray not.

What is your vision? Can you see the clear path God has set before you? Can you see past the distractions to where God is directing you? May your answers be yes, but make sure you have regular checkups.

His Promises

Your eye is a lamp that provides light for your body. When your eye is healthy, your whole body is filled with light.

MATTHEW 6:22

We don't look at the troubles we can see now; rather, we fix our gaze on things that cannot be seen. For the things we see now will soon be gone, but the things we cannot see will last forever.

2 CORINTHIANS 4:18

The Holy Spirit . . . will teach you everything and will remind you of everything I have told you.

JOHN 14:26

CLEAR AS MUD

Sometimes it's a real challenge to see God's will. Even when you're walking with Him by reading His Word on a regular basis, by being around other believers and bouncing ideas off of them, by going to God in prayer . . . sometimes it's just a real challenge.

It may be understanding where He is leading—which may not be clear at all. Or maybe it's clear, but it's something that is difficult and makes you uncomfortable—forgiving a friend who has wounded you, taking a step in faith to pursue another career, relocating to another city, or other stressful decisions of life.

When you are having difficulty knowing what to do, ask God to make it clear to you and then follow your heart—after all, He's the one who created you and gave you the passions you have.

And know this: clear or not, the Lord *is* leading . . . and *is* with you.

His Promises

Don't act thoughtlessly, but understand what the Lord wants you to do.
EPHESIANS 5:17

The LORD your God is living among you.
He is a mighty savior.
He will take delight in you with gladness.
With his love, he will calm all your fears.
He will rejoice over you with joyful songs.
ZEPHANIAH 3:17

This world is fading away, along with everything that people crave. But anyone who does what pleases God will live forever.
1 JOHN 2:17

RESOLVING DIFFERENCES WITH GRACE

It's human nature to let disagreements get personal, and too often people resort to name-calling, mockery, and personal attacks.

If you find yourself in a conflict with someone else, approach it as a positive opportunity, even if the other person doesn't see it that way yet. Agree to talk about the problem and emphasize that you want to focus not on each other but on the issue. Acknowledge that having different perspectives can be healthy. Make it clear that you value the other person's opinion and that you want a constructive resolution. Explore how you can get past the problem in a way that respects everyone involved. If you can focus on the principal interests, not the people, it can turn into a very constructive experience.

When you approach conflict this way, you'll

find it can be illuminating—a chance for all parties to grow or to see an issue more fully. If it's handled with respect for others' opinions and perspectives, it can have very positive results.

His Promises

Don't bother correcting mockers;
*   they will only hate you.*
But correct the wise,
*   and they will love you.*
Instruct the wise,
*   and they will be even wiser.*
Teach the righteous,
*   and they will learn even more.*

PROVERBS 9:8-9

Starting a quarrel is like opening a floodgate,
*   so stop before a dispute breaks out.*

PROVERBS 17:14

Never pay back evil with more evil. Do things in such a way that everyone can see you are honorable. Do all that you can to live in peace with everyone.

ROMANS 12:17-18

A WORTHY EXAMPLE

A career doesn't define who you are; it's simply what you do. Too many people find themselves pressured to make decisions that take them away from their goals rather than moving them toward them. Sometimes it's for financial reasons, sometimes it's due to family issues, and sometimes it's just the logistics of making a change. And while all of those are real factors, it's important to keep your goals in focus and remember that what you do should be an overflow of who you are. You were designed for a satisfying life.

Remember that the key is not what you do but who you are. You were meant to live as an imitator of Christ, sacrificing yourself for others as He did for you. More than anything else, that should drive your decisions about careers, relationships, and other commitments. Evaluate every opportunity not by how much money you can earn but by how effectively you can reflect Christ and live for Him in that situation.

His Promises

Imitate God, therefore, in everything you do, because you are his dear children. Live a life filled with love, following the example of Christ. He loved us and offered himself as a sacrifice for us, a pleasing aroma to God.

EPHESIANS 5:1-2

Anyone who belongs to Christ has become a new person. The old life is gone; a new life has begun!

2 CORINTHIANS 5:17

Throw off your old sinful nature and your former way of life, which is corrupted by lust and deception. Instead, let the Spirit renew your thoughts and attitudes. Put on your new nature, created to be like God—truly righteous and holy.

EPHESIANS 4:22-24

AN ANTIDOTE
FOR WORRY

Worry—it's what we do. No matter how brave a face we put on in certain situations, worry still nags at our hearts.

This issue of worry is mentioned numerous places in the Bible, so obviously it is important to God. And for good reason. Worry not only saps us of passion and energy, but it also drains us dry of our hope and trust in the God who created us.

The apostle Paul reminds us to stop and thank God for all He has done for us. If we remember what God has already done for us, we can hold on to the assurance that He will continue to provide and make a way through the uncertainty of tomorrow. It's lying back in the strong arms of God and basking in the peace that time with Him provides.

God will relieve you of worry if you ask Him. It doesn't always mean that instead of worry He will give you success or the outcome you think is best. What He does promise to give seems unfathomable to the world: peace.

His Promises

Don't worry about anything; instead, pray about everything. Tell God what you need, and thank him for all he has done. Then you will experience God's peace, which exceeds anything we can understand. His peace will guard your hearts and minds as you live in Christ Jesus.

PHILIPPIANS 4:6-7

Give all your worries and cares to God, for he cares about you.

1 PETER 5:7

Seek the Kingdom of God above all else, and live righteously, and he will give you everything you need. So don't worry about tomorrow, for tomorrow will bring its own worries. Today's trouble is enough for today.

MATTHEW 6:33-34

STRENGTH FOR THE WEARY

We've all been there. For me, it's been on the football field—or lately, riding my bike up a long, tough hill. For you, it may not be in an athletic environment, but we all know and have experienced enough to know that the uphill climbs are found everywhere in our lives.

Even "youths" and "young men" will grow tired—it's a part of the human condition. Maybe it's Mondays or at the end of the month or the quarter. Maybe it's after something has happened in your life to sap you of that last ounce of energy and "able to" that you were saving to get through the week. Sometimes week after week just gets to you.

It's easy to get worn down, emotionally and physically. We need to look to the Lord for rest and rejuvenation, which He promises.

His Promises

He gives power to the weak
and strength to the powerless.
Even youths will become weak and tired,
and young men will fall in exhaustion.
But those who trust in the LORD will find new
strength.
They will soar high on wings like eagles.
They will run and not grow weary.
They will walk and not faint.

ISAIAH 40:29-31

Think of all the hostility he endured from sin-
ful people; then you won't become weary and
give up.

HEBREWS 12:3

Deep in your hearts you know that every prom-
ise of the LORD your God has come true. Not
a single one has failed!

JOSHUA 23:14

MOVING ON

Life isn't trouble-free. Trouble often finds us, even if we're trying to avoid it. And for anyone who is pushing the envelope and maximizing their full potential, there's no guarantee that hardship won't show up too.

But so will the Lord, He promises. Life is hard, but God is good.

Each day seems to bring something new to each of us—sometimes we welcome whatever comes with open arms, and sometimes we do our best to hold it back. All of it can be used by God for our good and His glory; how it affects us depends in large part on whether we believe that or not.

God will always have a hold on us—no matter what we face.

His Promises

I have called you back from the ends of the earth,
*   saying, "You are my servant."*
For I have chosen you
*   and will not throw you away.*
Don't be afraid, for I am with you.
*   Don't be discouraged, for I am your God.*
I will strengthen you and help you.
*   I will hold you up with my victorious*
*   right hand.*

ISAIAH 41:9-10

"I will give you back your health
*   and heal your wounds," says the LORD.*

JEREMIAH 30:17

But all who listen to me will live in peace,
*   untroubled by fear of harm.*

PROVERBS 1:33

NO, THANKS;
I'M GOOD

Being content is not easy in the world of professional football. It seems like every year everyone expects more and more.

The same is true with our personal lives. We think that acquiring more and always replacing what we have with something bigger and better is the only way to find contentment.

Contentment is possible when you start with a grateful heart. Not a token sense of gratitude, but the realization that the Lord has blessed you with everything you need.

Notice the difference? The first approach says that something is missing in our lives and we need to get it. It's tough to be content when all we can think of is what we imagine everyone else has and we don't.

But when you approach everything in your

life with an attitude of gratitude, you will find contentment.

His Promises

Not that I was ever in need, for I have learned how to be content with whatever I have. I know how to live on almost nothing or with everything. I have learned the secret of living in every situation, whether it is with a full stomach or empty, with plenty or little.

PHILIPPIANS 4:11-12

Beware! Guard against every kind of greed. Life is not measured by how much you own.

LUKE 12:15

Whatever you do or say, do it as a representative of the Lord Jesus, giving thanks through him to God the Father.

COLOSSIANS 3:17

YOU ARE WHAT
YOU ABSORB

We absorb what is around us and reflect it back in different ways. Someone lets us pull out in front of them in traffic, and we wave someone else in a few moments later. Someone shares a word of encouragement or prayer with us, and when we return home, our spouse is the beneficiary of a kind word and a warm embrace.

What we take in often comes back in ways we can't anticipate. The key is to make sure that what we absorb is helpful to us and glorifying to God. It must demonstrate that we know our bodies and minds are God's temple, the dwelling place of the Holy Spirit.

That's why Coach Noll, our head coach when I was with the Pittsburgh Steelers, was always careful with the coaches and players he brought to the team. Because he was trying to create a positive atmosphere that would solidify us, he had to carefully screen the attitudes of everyone who was coming in.

What are you absorbing into your life today? Do you need to add more healthy things, eliminating things that compromise your witness and do not glorify God? The things that you take in often come out in your words, your attitudes, your habits. Make sure everything you bring in is worthy of being in the temple.

His Promises

You are not controlled by your sinful nature. You are controlled by the Spirit if you have the Spirit of God living in you. (And remember that those who do not have the Spirit of Christ living in them do not belong to him at all.) And Christ lives within you, so even though your body will die because of sin, the Spirit gives you life because you have been made right with God.

ROMANS 8:9-10

He is the Holy Spirit, who leads into all truth. The world cannot receive him, because it isn't looking for him and doesn't recognize him. But

*you know him, because he lives with you now
and later will be in you.*

JOHN 14:17

*Because you belong to him, the power of the life-
giving Spirit has freed you from the power of sin
that leads to death.*

ROMANS 8:2

DOUBTFUL

Life batters us at times. We can be banged around and buffeted by the ever-present winds of life—job changes (whether we want them or not), the frailty of our health or the health of our loved ones, rejection by friends, or another failed attempt on our part to do something we have long wanted to do.

Perhaps you've been fortunate and haven't experienced doubt in a while, though I doubt it. It hits us all on a regular basis, and it can be devastating when it hits—causing us to lose not only focus, but hope. The devil uses doubt to get us off track, to sap us of our energy for the day. When it comes, it rocks our world. That certainly has happened to me in my life.

But then Jesus comes to us to keep those doubts from taking firm root. He calls us to faith, to a belief that in the end, even when it doesn't always seem like it, we will prevail, we will win with Him.

Live as doubt-free as you can. And when doubts start to gather, honestly admit them to God.

His Promises

Blessed are those who believe without seeing me.
JOHN 20:29

If you need wisdom, ask our generous God, and he will give it to you. He will not rebuke you for asking. But when you ask him, be sure that your faith is in God alone.
JAMES 1:5-6

I have fought the good fight, I have finished the race, and I have remained faithful.
2 TIMOTHY 4:7

PAIN MANAGEMENT

Pain is a powerful teacher. None of us likes to learn life's lessons the hard way, but it's better than not learning them at all. We would rather not experience the pain of mistakes and failures, but the experience makes us stronger and teaches us valuable truths.

It's great when others can pass on to us the things they have learned, but many times their advice isn't enough. Most of us have to experience the hard lessons of life on our own for them to really sink in and become a part of our character.

Learn whatever you can from other people's mistakes. Let their pain become your teacher. But there will be times when your own pain is the only way to learn life's deepest lessons, and those are the ones that stick. Those who are wise will take every opportunity to learn from everything they experience.

His Promises

We know that God causes everything to work together for the good of those who love God and are called according to his purpose for them.

ROMANS 8:28

He will wipe every tear from their eyes, and there will be no more death or sorrow or crying or pain. All these things are gone forever.

REVELATION 21:4

What we suffer now is nothing compared to the glory he will reveal to us later.

ROMANS 8:18

THE LITTLE THINGS

God may call us to do some big things in our lives but being obedient to God in the little things He calls us to do on a day-to-day basis is critical. Too often we don't see the importance of the little things because they seem so insignificant. Or sometimes we are not sure that we can pull them off, so we end up stopping short of where we know God wants us to go.

How many victories in our lives are we missing because we fail to do the little things or we pull up just a couple of yards short? How many victories in our lives are just around the next corner, but we stop walking and never get to that corner?

God has an assignment for your life—it is perfect, and it is filled with purpose. Run the play to the end. Don't pull up short. Press through any obstacle that gets in your way.

His Promises

Joyful are people of integrity,
*   who follow the instructions of the LORD.*
Joyful are those who obey his laws
*   and search for him with all their hearts.*
They do not compromise with evil,
*   and they walk only in his paths.*

PSALM 119:1-3

Do not throw away this confident trust in the Lord. Remember the great reward it brings you!

HEBREWS 10:35

Though they stumble, they will never fall,
*   for the LORD holds them by the hand.*

PSALM 37:24

GOD IN
THE BRACKETS

Every spring, it happens—March Madness. The NCAA basketball tournament. A collection of extraordinary teams and games where the watchword is simply "survive and move on." The more you think about it, this basketball tournament is a lot like life—it's just about hanging on.

I'll bet there are times you can't see past the glare of problems blinding your eyes, when you don't feel like you deserve to see the light of a brand-new day. But I do know that there is someone who cares and whom God will use to open up a hole for daylight to shine on all the turmoil you are facing.

So no matter what's going on in your life, wait just a moment longer. Look around and you'll see them—people who are there for you.

Like a "Cinderella team" in the Final Four, it may be those you least expected. But they are sent by Someone who is always there for you.

His Promises

The Lord will deliver me from every evil attack and will bring me safely into his heavenly Kingdom. All glory to God forever and ever!
2 TIMOTHY 4:18

I know the LORD is always with me.
   I will not be shaken, for he is right beside me.
PSALM 16:8

Continue in the faith. . . . We must suffer many hardships to enter the Kingdom of God.
ACTS 14:22

EMPOWERING THE PEOPLE ABOVE YOU

Leadership isn't always about having the right answer or about telling others what to do. As a matter of fact, leadership is not about either of those things—there are plenty of smart, aggressive people who are very poor leaders. Instead, leadership—particularly the kind of leadership Christ exemplified and calls us to—is all about serving others. It's about helping them become better at whatever we are leading them in and helping them ultimately fulfill their potential in whatever setting they find themselves.

When I was coaching, I never asked anyone to do anything that I wasn't willing to do. I always made sure to clearly cast and keep before the team the vision of where we were going and the mission of how we were going to get there.

And I provided the resources the other coaches and players needed to get there.

But most important, I did everything I could to let them know I was there to serve them.

His Promises

Whoever wants to be a leader among you must be your servant, and whoever wants to be first among you must become your slave. For even the Son of Man came not to be served but to serve others and to give his life as a ransom for many.

MATTHEW 20:26-28

Be an example to all believers in what you say, in the way you live, in your love, your faith, and your purity.

1 TIMOTHY 4:12

Don't lord it over the people assigned to your care, but lead them by your own good example.

1 PETER 5:3

MAKING FAILURE
WORK FOR YOU

Part of what set Michael Jordan apart was his philosophy about being willing to take a risk. As Jordan said,

> I've missed more than 9,000 shots in my career. I've lost almost 300 games. Twenty-six times, I've been trusted to take the game-winning shot and missed. I've failed over and over and over again in my life. And that is why I succeed.

Babe Ruth struck out almost twice the number of times that he hit a home run, yet he is still considered one of the greats. Abraham Lincoln lost almost every political race he entered, until he was finally elected president of the United States.

We'll fall short. We'll fall down. We'll fail. That's one piece of life advice that we seem to forget to tell young people. So often they are confronted with failure in ways that they didn't expect.

When things happen to us that aren't exactly what we had hoped for, there are a number of ways we can respond. But there's only one response that will help us to move on toward the promise of a new day full of opportunities.

Get over it, get up, and try it again.

His Promises

Let us run with endurance the race God has set before us. We do this by keeping our eyes on Jesus, the champion who initiates and perfects our faith. . . . Think of all the hostility he endured from sinful people; then you won't become weary and give up.

HEBREWS 12:1-3

Don't you realize that in a race everyone runs, but only one person gets the prize? So run to win!

1 CORINTHIANS 9:24

The Lord isn't really being slow about his promise, as some people think. No, he is being patient for your sake. He does not want anyone to be destroyed, but wants everyone to repent.

2 PETER 3:9

BE PREPARED

The more we know about what we are doing, the more we can usually get people to listen.

I found that especially true in coaching. Players would listen because of the respect they needed to show initially to us as coaches. However, when it became apparent to a player that a coach didn't really know what he was talking about, the player tuned him out.

I always appreciated Coach Noll's approach. He wanted all of us on the Steelers staff to be sure that we understood what we were teaching the players. We were teachers first, and our goal was to prepare our players for as many situations as possible—to be able to think and be prepared for whatever might happen.

The same is true when God tells us to go out and speak about Him. He wants us to be ready when someone asks us why we believe what we believe. Why we accepted Jesus Christ into our lives. Why we follow Christ and try to live—hopefully it shows—as He wants us to live.

So be prepared. Any moment could be a time when He works through you to change a life for all eternity.

His Promises

If someone asks about your hope as a believer, always be ready to explain it. But do this in a gentle and respectful way. . . . Then if people speak against you, they will be ashamed when they see what a good life you live because you belong to Christ.

1 PETER 3:15-16

The LORD replied, "Don't say, 'I'm too young,' for you must go wherever I send you and say whatever I tell you. And don't be afraid of the people, for I will be with you and will protect you."

JEREMIAH 1:7-8

You will receive power when the Holy Spirit comes upon you. And you will be my witnesses, telling people about me everywhere—in Jerusalem, throughout Judea, in Samaria, and to the ends of the earth.

ACTS 1:8

HIS CHOICE

We are called by Christ to make disciples of all nations, but it's not all up to us. The remarkable fact is that God chose us to do this. He isn't surprised by what happened to us, and He won't be surprised by what might happen to others through us. We are to make the most of our opportunities, to grow and stretch in our faith, and to influence others to come to Christ. And in all of that, we are to trust God, guided by His Word, to not only be there as we walk through doors He is opening, but to realize that He is leading us through and encouraging us along the way.

God's Word is what is producing the fruit through the Holy Spirit, not our efforts. We are called to be God's messengers, God's ambassadors, while we are here. We are not called to be God. But He will use our humble efforts for good—His eternal good.

His Promises

You didn't choose me. I chose you. I appointed you to go and produce lasting fruit, so that the Father will give you whatever you ask for, using my name.

JOHN 15:16

It is the same with my word.
    I send it out, and it always produces fruit.
It will accomplish all I want it to,
    and it will prosper everywhere I send it.

ISAIAH 55:11

Never be ashamed to tell others about our Lord.

2 TIMOTHY 1:8

TRUST THE PLAY

Faith is a big component in a football team's game plan. If each player can depend on the others to carry out their assignments, the defense works effectively. If they don't have faith in their teammates, they abandon the plan and open up holes for the offense to exploit.

Running an offense requires faith too. A quarterback has to trust that the receiver will run his route correctly, and the receiver has to trust that the ball will arrive in the right place at the right time.

That's how life works too. We have to trust that the assignment God has given us is the right one. We need to know that the people and circumstances around us are running a pattern that will work out for good. We need to forsake our natural instincts and play our position, no matter how things look, and trust that the plan will work. As we carry out our assignments faithfully, the results will come. That's what it means to live by faith, not by sight.

His Promises

Those who know your name trust in you,
*   for you, O LORD, do not abandon those who*
*   search for you.*

PSALM 9:10

I pray that God, the source of hope, will fill you
completely with joy and peace because you trust
in him. Then you will overflow with confident
hope through the power of the Holy Spirit.

ROMANS 15:13

How joyful are those who fear the LORD
*   and delight in obeying his commands.*
Their children will be successful everywhere;
*   an entire generation of godly people will be*
*   blessed.*
They themselves will be wealthy,
*   and their good deeds will last forever.*

PSALM 112:1-3

CONTINUALLY CHECK YOUR PRIORITIES

Christ's priorities are different from the world's value system, and most of us have to reevaluate our priorities from time to time in order to line them up with what's truly valuable.

A life centered on Christ will help to free us from the uncertainty of our tomorrows and worries about success and achievements—what Solomon called "chasing after the wind." It will also redirect our focus toward what really matters. It will put finances, health, relationships, and our goals for the future in the right perspective. When we "chase after God" rather than chasing after the wind, we find that our relationship with Him rearranges our priorities.

It's never too late to put things in order and enjoy the blessings God has placed all around us—blessings like a beautiful sunset, the face of a newborn baby, the laugh of a child, or any other evidence of His work in our lives. Shifting our priorities will require some changes, and it isn't always easy. If we make Him the center of our lives, He changes our perspective and our purpose.

His Promises

Don't let the excitement of youth cause you to forget your Creator. Honor him in your youth before you grow old and say, "Life is not pleasant anymore." . . . Fear God and obey his commands, for this is everyone's duty. God will judge us for everything we do, including every secret thing, whether good or bad.

ECCLESIASTES 12:1, 13-14

Wherever your treasure is, there the desires of your heart will also be.

LUKE 12:34

What do you benefit if you gain the whole world but lose your own soul? Is anything worth more than your soul?

MARK 8:36-37

UNIQUELY YOU

Have you thought about all the events that led up to this moment in your life—why you're here, how you've been shaped, what caused you to read this book or seek God's plans for your life? Have you wondered how much of it is accidental or random and how much is designed?

God knew exactly where you would be right now and exactly what you would be like. He knew about your passions and gifts and the platform you have. In fact He was very purposeful in designing your life. He made you to be uniquely significant and to have an eternal impact on the world around you.

How would you live differently if you really believed that God had intentionally designed you to impact others? What steps of faith would you take if you knew He had already planned them? What would you attempt if you were fully convinced He was backing you? What impossible problems would suddenly seem possible to deal with?

Don't be afraid to try big things that fit with God's purposes. No problem is too big for Him to solve. That means no problem is too big for us to attempt to solve in His strength. We were designed for such purposes.

His Promises

"I know the plans I have for you," says the LORD. "They are plans for good and not for disaster, to give you a future and a hope."
JEREMIAH 29:11

Because of Christ and our faith in him, we can now come boldly and confidently into God's presence.
EPHESIANS 3:12

The LORD is my helper,
*   so I will have no fear.*
*   What can mere people do to me?*
HEBREWS 13:6

STARTING EVERY DAY

Do you want to do something that will dramatically change your life and the lives of others around you?

Spend some quiet time every morning with the God who created you.

Keep a pad and a pen with you. Have a Bible at hand—preferably one that is easy to understand. Maybe start reading a chapter or two each day from the Gospel of John.

Pray for a few minutes—remember, you're just talking to God. Make some notes on what crossed your mind while you were praying. You may think your mind wanders, but maybe God is telling you something He'll come back to later.

Moments spent with the Lord are always well spent. If you have never done it before, commit to ten minutes each morning to begin with. If you have been doing this on a regular basis, increase your time. I promise those few minutes will change your life.

His Promises

I have not departed from his commands,
but have treasured his words more than
daily food.

JOB 23:12

Remain in me, and I will remain in you. For a branch cannot produce fruit if it is severed from the vine, and you cannot be fruitful unless you remain in me.

Yes, I am the vine; you are the branches. Those who remain in me, and I in them, will produce much fruit. For apart from me you can do nothing. Anyone who does not remain in me is thrown away like a useless branch and withers. Such branches are gathered into a pile to be burned. But if you remain in me and my words remain in you, you may ask for anything you want, and it will be granted!

JOHN 15:4-7

Take delight in the LORD,
    and he will give you your heart's desires.
Commit everything you do to the LORD.
    Trust him, and he will help you.

PSALM 37:4-5

WHERE THE RUBBER MEETS THE ROAD

It's impossible to grow up in Michigan, as I did, and not know who Henry Ford was. I had relatives working at the Ford plants in Detroit and all around southern Michigan. In the 1960s and 1970s, the automobile industry was a major part of Michigan life.

Developing the first car involved overcoming significant challenges, not least of which was convincing people they needed it. Generally speaking, people had no idea what Henry Ford had created. It wasn't in their wildest imaginations. Little did folks know that what he had created would be such a benefit to them and their lifestyles.

It can be like that in business, where we don't see the opportunities before us for progress or growth or a way of doing something that could be a benefit to many.

It can also be like that with God's Word. So many people are blissfully ignorant of the abundant life that Christ is offering. They go through life, often going through the motions of church and worship without ever fully connecting to the source of power that is truly available to them, not thinking they are missing the peace, abundant life, and promises that flow from that power.

They know they need something but can't pinpoint what it is. Why not share with them what a relationship with Jesus Christ has added to your life? The benefits are even more valuable than a new car.

His Promises

I am leaving you with a gift—peace of mind and heart. And the peace I give is a gift the world cannot give. So don't be troubled or afraid.
JOHN 14:27

The LORD will guide you continually,
giving you water when you are dry
and restoring your strength.

You will be like a well-watered garden,
   like an ever-flowing spring.

ISAIAH 58:11

Use [your] money to do good. [You] should be
rich in good works and generous to those in need,
always being ready to share with others. By doing
this [you] will be storing up [your] treasure as a
good foundation for the future so that [you] may
experience true life.

1 TIMOTHY 6:18-19

A FRESH LOOK

Football coaches make lots of decisions, most often determined by watching lots of film.

It's customary for coaches to watch every play in a game at least two times: once from the sideline camera's angle and once from the end zone camera's angle.

Why? Added perspective.

From the sideline camera shot, you can't see the spacing of the offensive and defensive linemen, but it becomes very clear from the end zone camera. On the other hand, actual yardage is lost on the end zone camera angle but is apparent from the sidelines.

Life is like that as well. So often we'll view someone through our single-lens life experiences. But that's a skewed view. A person who may seem arrogant to us actually could be extremely shy, or a person who doesn't speak openly about their faith or has concerns about faith may have past experiences that make that understandable . . . if we try to understand.

God wants us to avoid making snap decisions about people without getting to know them. Our initial perspectives may be inaccurate pictures of who they are.

His Promises

People judge by outward appearance, but the LORD looks at the heart.

1 SAMUEL 16:7

Your own ears will hear him.
Right behind you a voice will say,
"This is the way you should go,"
whether to the right or to the left.

ISAIAH 30:21

But I, the LORD, search all hearts
and examine secret motives.
I give all people their due rewards,
according to what their actions deserve.

JEREMIAH 17:10

BE AN ENCOURAGER

Day-to-day living is tough and getting tougher. The number of people who need a word of encouragement and a lift in their lives is growing. It is our duty to be that voice and hand of encouragement to everyone we meet.

Think about all the friends and extended family you haven't seen or talked to in a while. Make a list of ten of those people. Then, within the next week, call each of them to catch up on each other's lives and in particular to find out how they are doing.

As you close the conversation, ask if there is anything you can do for them or anything you can pray about for them. If they are bold enough to mention something, be ready to do it. Then check in with them again in a month.

Once you begin with people you know,

expand your sphere of encouragement. Get to know people you run into on a regular basis: the grocery store cashier, the server at your favorite restaurant, your hairdresser or mechanic. Begin with a smile and small talk but be prepared if God wants you to do more.

His Promises

Let everything you say be good and helpful, so that your words will be an encouragement to those who hear them.
EPHESIANS 4:29

Let us not neglect our meeting together, as some people do, but encourage one another.
HEBREWS 10:25

May God, who gives this patience and encouragement, help you live in complete harmony with each other, as is fitting for followers of Christ Jesus.
ROMANS 15:5

PRICE CHECK

Why does Jesus always seem to be switching the price tags on our values? Clearly His values don't match those of a society bent on success, achievement, and winning for the sake of winning. His price tags are the right ones; we've switched them and misplaced our values.

Do you feel the stress and strain of misplaced price tags in your life? If so, maybe it's time to remember what's most important and focus on that. You'll notice that Jesus and society have two different value systems. He emphasized humility, hunger for truth and righteousness, and things that have eternal rather than temporary importance. Society emphasizes power, status, awards, fame, and wealth. Whose values would you rather follow? Stay focused on God's values, and help others see the folly in many of the world's values.

His Promises

No one can serve two masters. For you will hate one and love the other; you will be devoted to one and despise the other. You cannot serve God and be enslaved to money.

MATTHEW 6:24

If you are untrustworthy about worldly wealth, who will trust you with the true riches of heaven?

LUKE 16:11

If someone has enough money to live well and sees a brother or sister in need but shows no compassion—how can God's love be in that person?

1 JOHN 3:17

VISION KEEPERS

It's easy to lose sight of a goal—or to lose heart in trying to reach it—but occasional reminders can help. When I was coaching, after a loss, I would often remind the team that our short-term goals were still attainable and that we were still on track to reach our ultimate goal. When the team had been playing well, I would remind them not to fall in love with their own press clippings but to remember that both pride and complacency were enemies to our mission and would eventually lead to a fall. Whether we were winning or losing, we had to shake off the past and keep moving ahead. We just needed to focus on the task right in front of us.

It's easy to put our heads down and forget why we do what we do, but keeping our eyes on the prize can keep us going. This is especially important when circumstances are bleak and discouragement sets in, but it's also true when things are going well and complacency sets in. Both situations tempt us to lose our focus. But when we remember where we're headed, we tend to have more success getting there.

His Promises

Where there is no vision, the people perish.
PROVERBS 29:18, KJV

You should finish what you started. Let the eagerness you showed in the beginning be matched now by your giving.
2 CORINTHIANS 8:11

I am certain that God, who began the good work within you, will continue his work until it is finally finished on the day when Christ Jesus returns.
PHILIPPIANS 1:6

DEEP AND HIGH

Almost all of us in the United States have been blessed financially, at least when compared to the rest of the world.

But living the Christian life is not about basking in the world's accolades, in whatever form they may come. It's not about how many material possessions we accumulate or how important we may be considered in the world's eyes. Instead, it is about how we maximize what God has given us on behalf of others, or as former NFL player and sports analyst James Brown put it in his book *Role of a Lifetime*, "recognizing the opportunities [we] have each day to add value to the lives around [us] and to make a difference in [our] world."

We should use our money for good, storing up treasures in heaven, finding ways to share with those in need.

God isn't keeping track of the amount of money you give; He's more concerned about your heart and your willingness to give in the first place.

His Promises

Those who are rich in this world . . . should be rich in good works and generous to those in need, always being ready to share with others. By doing this they will be storing up their treasure as a good foundation for the future so that they may experience true life.

1 TIMOTHY 6:17-19

Remember this—a farmer who plants only a few seeds will get a small crop. But the one who plants generously will get a generous crop.

2 CORINTHIANS 9:6

Sell your possessions and give to those in need. This will store up treasure for you in heaven! And the purses of heaven never get old or develop holes. Your treasure will be safe; no thief can steal it and no moth can destroy it.

LUKE 12:33

NO MATTER WHAT, DON'T GIVE UP

When things become difficult in our lives, we may want to throw our hands in the air and give up.

Don't.

There will be times when we'll want to simply stop and let someone else do what we know God has asked us to do.

Don't.

As followers of Christ, we are called to "press on to reach the end of the race and receive the heavenly prize for which God, through Christ Jesus, is calling us."

Set your course for things much larger than yourself by refusing to give up, and in doing so, direct the paths of those around you by passion and example.

His Promises

I don't mean to say that I have already achieved these things or that I have already reached perfection. But I press on to possess that perfection for which Christ Jesus first possessed me.

PHILIPPIANS 3:12

Be strong and courageous, for your work will be rewarded.

2 CHRONICLES 15:7

I press on to reach the end of the race and receive the heavenly prize for which God, through Christ Jesus, is calling us.

PHILIPPIANS 3:14

WORK WITH WHAT YOU'VE GOT

The Lord asks us to have faith. Faith in His Promises. Faith in His Son Jesus Christ. Faith in the hope of the resurrection of Christ. Faith in everything He has set forth in His Word.

He asks us to believe without doubting, to ask without stopping, to seek until we find, to knock because the door will be opened, and to pray without ceasing, believing that what we ask for, seek for, knock for, and pray for He will do something about.

But God also realizes that sometimes it's tough to believe. Sometimes we feel like Thomas, asking for physical proof of Jesus' resurrection. Sometimes we want to get our finite brains around an infinite God and understand things without having to do it on faith alone.

And usually those times are when we need to

have faith even more. Often it's in those times that the world keeps preying on us and nothing feels right. The disciples had their moments of doubt, and Jesus was standing there, right in front of them. So we don't need to feel guilty when we have our moments of doubt. Those are the days when we need to remember even more to just hang on and have faith. Even faith as small as a mustard seed.

That's all we need. God will take care of the rest.

His Promises

I tell you the truth, if you have faith and don't doubt, you can do things like this and much more. You can even say to this mountain, "May you be lifted up and thrown into the sea," and it will happen.

MATTHEW 21:21

We live by believing and not by seeing.

2 CORINTHIANS 5:7

I am convinced that nothing can ever separate us from God's love. Neither death nor life, neither angels nor demons, neither our fears for today nor our worries about tomorrow—not even the powers of hell can separate us from God's love. No power in the sky above or in the earth below—indeed, nothing in all creation will ever be able to separate us from the love of God that is revealed in Christ Jesus our Lord.

ROMANS 8:38-39

PERSEVERING
TO THE END

How often have you seen a team jump out to a big lead and then change what they were doing? The game isn't over, and suddenly they move to a different offense or defense, thinking that the game is already won.

Before you know it, the team who was behind scores two or three touchdowns, and all of a sudden, they have made what seemed like a lopsided loss into a competitive game. You'd think they would continue to play the same tough defense that had been successful— persevering until the game was won. But they don't. And they lose.

Stay strong until the end of the fight so that someday you can stand face-to-face with God and say that you persevered to the end! And then you'll hear, "Well done, good and faithful servant!"

The prize isn't for accomplishments; it's for "remaining faithful." We can't earn it or achieve it, no matter how many wins we have or all the earthly rewards that come with them.

The ultimate prize is the crown of righteousness that He will give us when He returns.

His Promises

I have fought the good fight, I have finished the race, and I have remained faithful. And now the prize awaits me—the crown of righteousness, which the Lord, the righteous Judge, will give me on the day of his return. And the prize is not just for me but for all who eagerly look forward to his appearing.

2 TIMOTHY 4:7-8

My life is worth nothing to me unless I use it for finishing the work assigned me by the Lord Jesus—the work of telling others the Good News about the wonderful grace of God.

ACTS 20:24

Above all, you must live as citizens of heaven, conducting yourselves in a manner worthy of the Good News about Christ. Then, whether I come and see you again or only hear about you, I will know that you are standing together with one spirit and one purpose, fighting together for the faith, which is the Good News.

PHILIPPIANS 1:27

REFUGE ANYWHERE, ANYTIME

The world has certainly seen its share of pandemics, surging waters, and crumbling mountains lately. Whether we have been in the midst of a natural disaster or not, if we reflect upon our own lives, we'd have to admit that we have experienced plenty of tumultuous and raging storms of all kinds. And yet, we went through them knowing that God is there to be our refuge and strength, an ever-present help in all our times of need.

What have you been in the midst of this past week? What are you facing that you are certain you cannot overcome or get around or through? What tragedy has hit that you never saw coming? What will you do with your child who seems to have lost his or her way?

Today and every day, turn to the one who

truly is your refuge and strength and always ready to help in times of trouble—God the Father Almighty! He will free you from all your fears.

His Promises

God is our refuge and strength,
always ready to help in times of trouble.

PSALM 46:1

The LORD is good,
a strong refuge when trouble comes.
He is close to those who trust in him.

NAHUM 1:7

O storm-battered city,
troubled and desolate!
I will rebuild you with precious jewels
and make your foundations from lapis lazuli

ISAIAH 54:11

LEAP OF FAITH

At times when life feels a bit bleak—when we have suffered the loss of a family member, when our jobs seem to be in danger or are already gone with no prospects on the immediate horizon, or when our children are making bad and dangerous choices—we need to be encouraging one another with the promise of the Resurrection.

The more bits of information we have about how our own resurrection will occur and how and when Christ will return, the more assured we are of it happening. That's how our minds work—seeing tends to enhance believing. The more information and historical or scientific facts we have at our disposal to substantiate what the Bible says, the more likely we are to take that leap of faith into the waiting arms of God.

Countless books have been published on the subject, but at the end of the day, believing in the promise of the resurrection and eternity still requires faith. The good news is, faith is all you really need.

His Promises

No eye has seen, no ear has heard,
*   and no mind has imagined*
what God has prepared
*   for those who love him.*

1 CORINTHIANS 2:9

If you openly declare that Jesus is Lord and believe in your heart that God raised him from the dead, you will be saved. For it is by believing in your heart that you are made right with God, and it is by openly declaring your faith that you are saved.

ROMANS 10:9-10

I am the resurrection and the life. Anyone who believes in me will live, even after dying.

JOHN 11:25

THE HEART OF
ALL THINGS

The heart reflects to the world who we are—the inner character we display outwardly. It's the quarterback of the soul, guiding the decisions we make and dictating what we choose to leave behind or take with us on the journey. Our heart sets the course of every day of our lives.

In our relationships, the state of our hearts will reveal how we view those around us. Do we see people in terms of their roles and responsibilities, or do we deal with their hearts as special creations of God? Can we look past the externals and see them as they really are?

The condition of our hearts will set the tone for all our relationships—including our relationship with God. It's the lens we look through. Our perceptions of God and others are based more on ourselves and our expectations than on our hearts. No wonder Jesus said a pre-requisite for seeing God is having a pure heart. And no wonder Proverbs 4:23 tells us to guard our hearts above all else. In the Kingdom of God and in all our relationships, the heart matters.

His Promises

God blesses those whose hearts are pure, for they will see God.

MATTHEW 5:8

Create in me a clean heart, O God.
    Renew a loyal spirit within me.

PSALM 51:10

I will give you a new heart, and I will put a new spirit in you.

EZEKIEL 36:26

FOR US

How many times have you prayed for a certain outcome, imagined that a problem has only one solution, and lost heart when that outcome or solution didn't occur?

And then you learn, of course, that God has something much better in store.

The year 2001 was a monster of a year in Tampa Bay. We rallied from a slow start to make the playoffs, only to lose to the Eagles. And then, despite much prayer, I was fired. That was not the answer or outcome I was looking for, but it was the answer I got. And so in the midst of much disappointment and uncertainty for the future, I packed up, not knowing what doors the Lord would open tomorrow, but still believing He would provide.

And He did. The Indianapolis Colts called

with a mission statement they wanted me to fulfill.

Once again I was reminded that in every outcome—whether it was the one I had been praying and hoping for or not—God had a good plan in place, something whereby He would be glorified.

His Promises

If God is for us, who can ever be against us?
ROMANS 8:31

How do you know what your life will be like tomorrow? Your life is like the morning fog—it's here a little while, then it's gone. What you ought to say is, "If the Lord wants us to, we will live and do this or that."
JAMES 4:14-15

The LORD directs the steps of the godly.
*   He delights in every detail of their lives.*
PSALM 37:23

PRAY TELL

Is public prayer a witness or an act of pride? Or is it something else—like an act of love and affection?

It depends entirely on the state of our hearts as to why we pray—whether it is in public or private. If we thank God for our blessings on a regular basis, we don't need to stop doing it when we're out in public. If, however, our motivation for praying in public is to be seen and to demonstrate to others that we pray to God, then maybe we've got a problem. And if it's about us—well, then, it probably is not about God.

After all, praying is merely speaking with God, spending time with Him. But praying to God is also, and most importantly, an act of love and affection. Praying to God is an act of trust in the one who gives us life. Praying to God is an act of humble surrender to the one who is in charge of it all and who created it all. If that's where our focus stays, then these other thoughts shouldn't matter. If we're worried about what others are thinking of our words or whether we are being watched, then our focus has changed.

His Promises

When you pray, don't be like the hypocrites who love to pray publicly on street corners and in the synagogues where everyone can see them. I tell you the truth, that is all the reward they will ever get. But when you pray, go away by yourself, shut the door behind you, and pray to your Father in private. Then your Father, who sees everything, will reward you.

MATTHEW 6:5-6

Pray in the Spirit at all times and on every occasion. Stay alert and be persistent in your prayers for all believers everywhere.

EPHESIANS 6:18

Pray like this:
    Our Father in heaven,
            may your name be kept holy.
    May your Kingdom come soon.
    May your will be done on earth,
            as it is in heaven.
    Give us today the food we need,
    and forgive us our sins,
            as we have forgiven those who sin
                    against us.
    And don't let us yield to temptation,
            but rescue us from the evil one.

MATTHEW 6:9-13

CHEER UP!

Christians can be some of the most dour people on the planet.

We claim to be called to serve the God who was the architect of the beauty all around us; yet we act and appear at times as if we have nothing to wake up to.

Here's the saddest part of the whole thing: It doesn't have to happen. Times can get tough. But as followers of and believers in Jesus Christ—if we have asked Him into our lives— we have the joy and hope of the Lord of lords and the King of kings in our lives. A joy that can overcome whatever we face. A joy that leads us into all the fullness of our future with Him in eternity.

Let it out! Let the joy out! Let the source of your joy—Jesus Christ—shine through you to the world around you. Let the joy, love, and power of the God of the universe flow through you so that others see a twinkle in your eyes, a smile on your face, and laughter in your voice.

Then they'll see Him! And He is the one they'll be attracted to!

His Promises

You love him even though you have never seen him. Though you do not see him now, you trust him; and you rejoice with a glorious, inexpressible joy.

1 PETER 1:8

Shout with joy to the LORD, all the earth!
    Worship the LORD with gladness.
    Come before him, singing with joy.
Acknowledge that the LORD is God!
    He made us, and we are his.
    We are his people, the sheep of his pasture.
Enter his gates with thanksgiving;
    go into his courts with praise.
    Give thanks to him and praise his name.
For the LORD is good.
    His unfailing love continues forever,

*and his faithfulness continues to each
generation*

PSALM 100:1-5

*People should eat and drink and enjoy the fruits
of their labor, for these are gifts from God.*

ECCLESIASTES 3:13

PROTECTIVE PADDING

I'm sure you've seen photos of early football players wearing those distinctive leather helmets. We've certainly come a long way since then with football gear, that's for sure.

But more important than protective sports equipment is the spiritual armor to prepare us for the spiritual battle we're engaged in each and every day.

We are engaged in a monumental battle for our souls between the forces of good, with God in command, and the forces of evil under Satan's power.

No wonder we need the full-body armor of God: the belt of truth and the body armor of God's righteousness (Ephesians 6:14); shoes of peace (verse 15); the shield of faith (verse 16);

the helmet of salvation and the sword of the Spirit, which is the Word of God (verse 17).

The good news is that in the very end, God wins. But we have work to do for Him in the meantime, so suit up!

His Promises

Put on all of God's armor so that you will be able to stand firm against all strategies of the devil. For we are not fighting against flesh-and-blood enemies, but against evil rulers and authorities of the unseen world. . . . Therefore, put on every piece of God's armor so you will be able to resist the enemy in the time of evil. Then after the battle you will still be standing firm.

EPHESIANS 6:11-13

Let us who live in the light be clearheaded, protected by the armor of faith and love, and wearing as our helmet the confidence of our salvation.

1 THESSALONIANS 5:8

In that coming day
no weapon turned against you will succeed.
You will silence every voice
raised up to accuse you.

These benefits are enjoyed by the servants of the
        LORD;
    their vindication will come from me.
    I, the LORD, have spoken!

ISAIAH 54:17

STARTING OVER
ON MONDAY

Every Monday morning during the season, most teams in the NFL do the same thing—they begin to plan for the next game. Sunday's game may have been a big win or a crushing loss, but teams don't have time to continue a celebration or wallow in disappointment. Another game is coming soon.

Our lives are a lot like that. We win big victories, make huge mistakes, experience deep joys, and suffer crippling disappointments. Whatever the case, we have to look forward.

That can be especially difficult when things aren't going well, and we have worries about our relationships, our kids, our finances, our dreams, or much more. People and circumstances let us down. But God doesn't, and He is sovereign over all of it.

When we begin the "Monday mornings" of our lives with a focus on God's game plan rather than our own, we'll be much more effective. We can look back over situations we have come through and learn from our mistakes, but there's never a need to dwell on them. And we can look toward the future and plan, but we can never control what happens. If we walk with God, following however He leads, we'll always be headed in the right direction.

His Promises

I know the LORD is always with me.
I will not be shaken, for he is right beside me.
No wonder my heart is glad, and I rejoice.
My body rests in safety.
For you will not leave my soul among the dead
or allow your holy one to rot in the grave.
You will show me the way of life,
granting me the joy of your presence
and the pleasures of living with you forever.

PSALM 16:8-11

Don't be impressed with your own wisdom.
Instead, fear the LORD and turn away
from evil.

Then you will have healing for your body
and strength for your bones.

PROVERBS 3:7-8

He has given me a new song to sing,
a hymn of praise to our God.
Many will see what he has done and be amazed.
They will put their trust in the LORD.

PSALM 40:3

THE OUTSIDE REFLECTING THE INSIDE

When I took over the Indianapolis Colts, I came preaching a manner of football that was slightly different from what they had played before.

On offense, I wanted us to focus on taking care of the ball—no turnovers. That meant being less aggressive than they were used to.

Similarly, on defense, our scheme was predicated on taking care of each person's responsibility, sometimes by "staying at home."

During that first year, we made the playoffs, but a 41–0 playoff loss showed our guys' actions didn't mirror their words.

It's not that they didn't mean well or weren't being truthful, but in their core, their beliefs didn't quite match up, so in crucial situations they would revert to old habits.

Ultimately, our actions really do indicate the

state of our hearts as well as the extent of our faith in the living God. If we truly believe that we are seeking God and His will for our lives, that should be reflected in how we conduct ourselves on a daily basis.

His Promises

I know all the things you do. I have seen your love, your faith, your service, and your patient endurance. And I can see your constant improvement in all these things.
REVELATION 2:19

Therefore, since we have been made right in God's sight by faith, we have peace with God because of what Jesus Christ our Lord has done for us. Because of our faith, Christ has brought us into this place of undeserved privilege where we now stand, and we confidently and joyfully look forward to sharing God's glory.
ROMANS 5:1-2

By his divine power, God has given us everything we need for living a godly life. We have received all of this by coming to know him, the one who called us to himself by means of his marvelous glory and excellence. And because of his glory and excellence, he has given us great and precious promises.

2 PETER 1:3-4

MORE THAN THE WORLD OFFERS

What is really important in life? Do we chase the world's fortunes and accolades at the expense of our own spiritual welfare? Too often the answer to the second question is yes, and that response takes care of the answer to the first question. We can't really deny it, but we can work to change that way of life before it's too late.

Spend more quiet time with God. Read Scripture and other devotional materials more. Spend more time in prayer, and seek advice, encouragement, and prayer from others you trust.

Focus on spiritual things, and become more intentional about doing things for others, spending time with your family, and looking for opportunities to be a role model to others in your community.

Remember, who you are is not defined by worldly "stuff" but by your heart for God.

So make a habit of doing good for others, and in the process, you will glorify God.

His Promises

What do you benefit if you gain the whole world but lose your own soul? Is anything worth more than your soul?

MATTHEW 16:26

Work hard to show the results of your salvation, obeying God with deep reverence and fear. For God is working in you, giving you the desire and the power to do what pleases him.

PHILIPPIANS 2:12-13

Now may the God of peace make you holy in every way, and may your whole spirit and soul and body be kept blameless until our Lord Jesus Christ comes again.

1 THESSALONIANS 5:23

About the Authors

TONY DUNGY is the #1 *New York Times* best-selling author of *Quiet Strength*, *Uncommon*, *The Mentor Leader*, *The One Year Uncommon Life Daily Challenge*, and *Uncommon Marriage* (with Lauren Dungy). He led the Indianapolis Colts to Super Bowl victory on February 4, 2007, the first such win for an African American head coach. Dungy established another NFL first by becoming the first head coach to lead his teams to the playoffs for ten consecutive years. He retired from coaching in 2009 and now serves as a studio analyst for NBC's *Football Night in America*. He is dedicated to mentoring others, especially young people, and encouraging them to live uncommon lives. The Dungys are the parents of eleven children.

NATHAN WHITAKER holds degrees from Duke University, Harvard Law School, and the University of Florida, and has worked in football administration for the Tampa Bay Buccaneers. He has written multiple *New York Times* bestsellers and lives with his family in Florida.

DARE TO BE UNCOMMON

UNCOMMON
Softcover (978-1-4143-2682-5)
Audio CDs read by Tony Dungy (978-1-4143-2683-2)

UNCOMMON MARRIAGE
Hardcover (978-1-4143-8369-9)
Audio CDs read by Tony and Lauren Dungy (978-1-4143-8371-2)

UNCOMMON MARRIAGE BIBLE STUDY
Softcover (978-1-4143-9199-1)

THE ONE YEAR UNCOMMON LIFE DAILY CHALLENGE
Softcover (978-1-4143-4828-5)
Deluxe LeatherLike edition (978-1-4143-6248-9)

UNCOMMON MANHOOD
Hardcover (978-1-4143-6707-1)
Four-color gift book adapted from *Uncommon.* A perfect gift for Father's Day!

DARE TO BE UNCOMMON
DVD curriculum led by Tony Dungy (978-1-4143-6705-7)

VISIT WWW.COACHDUNGY.COM